At ✻ Issue

Cosmetic Surgery

Kristen Bailey, *Book Editor*

Bruce Glassman, *Vice President*
Bonnie Szumski, *Publisher*
Helen Cothran, *Managing Editor*

GREENHAVEN PRESS
An imprint of Thomson Gale, a part of The Thomson Corporation

THOMSON
✻
GALE

Detroit • New York • San Francisco • San Diego • New Haven, Conn.
Waterville, Maine • London • Munich

For more information, contact
Greenhaven Press
27500 Drake Rd.
Farmington Hills, MI 48331-3535
Or you can visit our Internet site at http://www.gale.com

LIBRARY OF CONGRESS CATALOGING-IN-PUBLICATION DATA
Cosmetic surgery / Kristen Bailey, book editor.
p. cm. — (At issue)
Includes bibliographical references and index.
ISBN 0-7377-3107-9 (lib. : alk. paper) — ISBN 0-7377-3108-7 (pbk. : alk. paper)
1. Body, Human—Social aspects. 2. Surgery, Plastic—Social aspects. I. Bailey, Kristen. II. At issue (San Diego, Calif.)
HM636.C68 2005
617.9'5—dc22   2005040238

Printed in the United States of America

Contents

Page

Introduction   4

1. Cosmetic Surgery Helps Children with Birth Defects   7
   Kathleen Magee and William Magee

2. Increasing Numbers of American Men Are Getting   14
   Cosmetic Surgery
   Bill Troy

3. Thousands of Asians Are Turning to Cosmetic Surgery   19
   Lisa Takeuchi Cullen

4. Smooth Operations   30
   Allison Samuels

5. The Desire to Look Young Is the Main Reason People   33
   Seek Cosmetic Surgery
   Courtney Lomax

6. Women's Magazines Drive the Demand for Cosmetic   38
   Surgery
   Deborah A. Sullivan

7. Patients Can Become Addicted to Cosmetic Surgery   49
   Virginia L. Blum

8. Reality TV Shows About Cosmetic Surgery Reveal   60
   Americans' Self-Absorption
   Psychology Today

9. Teenagers Should Wait Until They Are Adults to   64
   Undergo Cosmetic Surgery
   Jae-Ha Kim

10. Doctors Need to Follow Stricter Guidelines in   67
    Choosing Cosmetic Surgery Patients
    Kimberly Shearer Palmer

Organizations to Contact   71

Bibliography   74

Index   77

Introduction

In January 2004 best-selling author Olivia Goldsmith died from complications of cosmetic surgery to remove loose skin from her chin. Statistics on the number of people who die from cosmetic surgery are difficult to estimate because the cause of many of these deaths are documented as respiratory failure or heart attack. However, according to the journal *Plastic and Reconstructive Surgery*, one in five thousand people die each year from liposuction procedures alone. This statistic is particularly alarming given that the odds of dying from other types of surgery are approximately one in two hundred thousand. Other risks of cosmetic surgery include brain damage, temporary paralysis, infection, blood clots, nerve damage, chronic pain, scarring, and other undesirable results.

Despite the risks, people are undergoing cosmetic surgery in record numbers. Approximately 8.7 million people underwent cosmetic surgery in 2003, a 32 percent increase over 2002, according to statistics released by the American Society of Plastic Surgeons (ASPS). Among these cosmetic surgery patients are more and more young people. According to the American Society for Aesthetic Plastic Surgery (ASAPS), the number of girls eighteen and younger who underwent plastic surgery in 2003 was nearly triple the number of patients in that age group the year before.

Many of these people, young and old, who are choosing to have cosmetic surgery may be succumbing to perceived pressures from society. By opening nearly any magazine or watching television for just a few moments, it is impossible to miss the standardized ideal of what is considered beautiful in American society. A pretty, symmetrical face, a thin frame, and sizable breasts complete the perceived norm of an attractive woman.

Men, too, can feel pressure to have a youthful, fit appearance. However, according to the American Academy of Facial and Plastic Reconstructive Surgeons survey, men are much more likely than women to desire cosmetic surgery for work-related reasons. In a survey reported by MSNBC, men are 15 percent more likely than women to seek cosmetic surgery because they feel an improved appearance will help them in their career. Despite the cost and the risks, men often view cosmetic surgery as an investment toward their future success. According to ASPS president James Wells, "people are willing to make an investment in themselves to achieve the look they want."

Both women and men who have just been divorced or left by a partner may seek out surgery to give their egos a boost after being rejected. Others may fear that they will be rejected in the future by a spouse or partner and will try to appear more youthful or attractive in order to "save" their relationship. Some patients seek cosmetic surgery if a partner or spouse has suggested that they should improve their appearance. Of course, as Los Angeles plastic surgeon Peter B. Fodor, president of the American Society for Aesthetic Plastic Surgery points out, "nobody should undergo plastic surgery at someone else's suggestion."

Some people want to achieve the physical ideal of the dominant culture. For example, a dramatic cosmetic procedure for leg-lengthening is becoming popular in China, the *Lancet* medical journal reports. Doctors are offering plastic surgery that "stretches" the leg bones and can add ten centimeters to a person's height, which is socially important in China. Height is sometimes even listed among the criteria on job postings. Many law schools require that women be at least five feet one and men over five feet five for admission. Although the surgery can improve people's chances for jobs and marriage, some patients have suffered serious, crippling complications. In some cultures the physical ideal is inextricably linked with moral beliefs about sexuality. In non-Western societies such as Morocco and Egypt that prize virginity in brides to be, female patients occasionally have cosmetic surgery on their hymens to "restore" their virginity and avoid social persecution.

People may also seek cosmetic surgery because they have seen or learned about it on television. In the past few years reality television series that depict cosmetic surgery, such as *The Swan* on Fox and *Extreme Makeover* on ABC, have proliferated. While many plastic surgeons have complained that reality television shows present an unrealistic picture of cosmetic surgery, the shows have succeeded in bringing surgery into the minds and homes of millions of people who may have never considered it before. According to Garth Fisher, a surgeon who has performed operations on *Extreme Makeover*, the shows have helped people to become more aware of plastic surgery and its benefits. "Every day we operate on people and we change people's lives," says Fisher, a board-certified plastic surgeon practicing in Beverly Hills, California, "This is really an opportunity for America to see what we see every day in our practice."

On the other hand, some people feel that people's happiness should not rely so heavily on their appearance. According to author Christine Rosen, "cosmetic surgery might make individual people happier, but in the aggregate it makes life worse for everyone . . . the pressure to conform to these elevated standards increases. So, too, does the amount of time and money we spend on what is ultimately a futile goal: cheating time." In a *Focus on the Family* article author David Wall also criticizes what he considers the excessive emphasis on appearance. He notes, "Our society is narcissistically obsessed with physical perfection as the road to ultimate fulfillment."

Although there are risks, millions of people undergo cosmetic surgery each year and are happy and satisfied with their new selves. As more and more people seek the newest cosmetic procedures that are rapidly becoming available, the debate over cosmetic surgery will continue. The viewpoints in *At Issue: Cosmetic Surgery* focus on the many issues involved in this debate, including surgery addiction, the role of the media, and the dangers and benefits of surgery.

1

Cosmetic Surgery Helps Children with Birth Defects

Kathleen Magee and William Magee

Kathleen Magee, a clinical social worker, and her husband, William Magee, a physician, are the cofounders of Operation Smile. Operation Smile is a private, not-for-profit volunteer medical services organization that provides free cosmetic and reconstructive surgery and related health care services to impoverished children and young adults throughout the world.

While many teenagers pore over magazines, dreaming about cosmetic surgery to perfect their noses or enhance their bustlines, some people's desire for cosmetic surgery goes beyond simple vanity. When Kathleen Magee and her husband, William Magee, visited the Philippines with a medical team in 1981, they encountered numerous children with facial deformities who had a real need for cosmetic surgery but could not afford it. Although they were able to operate on and help many of the children, they still had to turn away many more. They were inspired by this experience to organize a team of doctors to provide reconstructive surgery and general medical assistance to poor children around the world. Today their organization, Operation Smile, helps thousands of children each year.

Although many young people are concerned about acne and dieting, there are some children who retreat from social contact because of facial deformities that can be changed only through surgery. Operation Smile is an organization dedicated to giving young people who are suffering from physical disfigurement an opportunity to come out of hiding and become active members of their community. This organization received the Kellogg's Hannah Neil World of Children Award, an annual $100,000 prize honoring those who make significant contributions in the world of children.

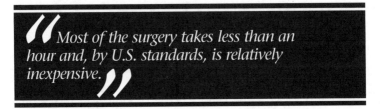

Most of the surgery takes less than an hour and, by U.S. standards, is relatively inexpensive.

Operation Smile is a private, nonprofit volunteer medical-service organization that helps children in developing countries and the United States who are in need of reconstructive surgery. Funding for Operation Smile comes from individuals, businesses, and foundations. There are 26 chapters in the United States and 18 international foundations, all of which help raise money or seek outright gifts of anything from diapers to surgical equipment and supplies. International mission trips airlift medical supplies and teams of medical volunteers for 2-week stints to hospitals in developing areas of Europe, Africa, Asia, Central and South America, and the Middle East.

The Beginning

When Kathleen Magee and her husband, Dr. William Magee, visited the Philippines in 1981 with a medical team, they were astonished at the number of children with facial deformities. The plastic surgeons and their assistants were able to operate on 150 children in three cities in 5 days but had to turn away nearly twice that number of patients. This incident inspired Kathleen, a clinical social worker, to make plans to organize another team of doctors and medical assistants to return to the Philippines the following year. They raised money to finance the trip through bake sales and solicitation of donations of medical supplies. On this second trip they again had to turn away more patients. It was on the heels of that second trip in 1982 that they organized Operation Smile, which has served more than 53,000 children worldwide through reconstructive surgery and general medical assistance. In addition, Operation Smile also provides medical training and continuing education for health-care professionals wherever its staff and volunteer medical personnel visit.

Most of the surgery takes less than an hour and, by U.S. standards, is relatively inexpensive. The medical teams repair cleft palates, cleft lips, burns, tumors, and other birth defects, all without cost to the patient. Most surgery is performed on children, but sometimes adults are helped as well.

Project Stories

Tina. In severe cases, the patient is brought to the United States for a series of surgical procedures, as was the case for Tina. Because of a baseball-sized hernia of brain tissue that covered her nose, Tina had spent the first 15 years of her life in isolation in her Philippine village. Embarrassed that their child was an oddity, Tina's parents sheltered her for many years. When her father heard about a possible opportunity for his daughter to have surgery to remove the unsightly growth, he quickly investigated it. He was told that a group of U.S. surgeons could help his daughter look "normal." Father and daughter traveled to the United States and between surgeries were able to explore the area. When the medical procedures were complete and all looked well, they were given the opportunity to remain in the United States so Tina could complete her education and possibly go on to college. Because the village had given so much support to the family, the father refused to stay. "Now we must go home and give back to our community," he said. Tina continued her education in her homeland and graduated as valedictorian of her high school class. Not only did the surgery restore her natural beauty, she was confident in her ability to learn and share her skills with those who had given her so much support.

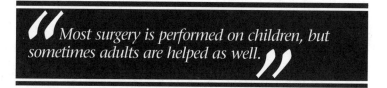

Most surgery is performed on children, but sometimes adults are helped as well.

Jose. Another person from the Philippines who benefited from Operation Smile was Jose, who had a 2-pound tumor on his jaw. When the tumor was removed, his jaw and the inside of his mouth needed to be rebuilt, which the team did by using bones from his ribs. Jose is now a spokesperson for the organization, telling people about his experience, training others to give talks, and raising money for Operation Smile.

Closer to Home

Because of the nature of this type of surgery, some U.S. insurance companies will not cover the cost and, in many cases, no insurance coverage has been provided for the patient through the parent's employment. Children who are referred by the public schools or community service organizations go through a screening process, after which a participating hospital is identified and volunteer medical professionals perform the surgery at the hospital. In the United States, 260 applicants were evaluated for treatment in November and December of 1999, at 10 sites from Boston to Salt Lake City. At the time this article was written, 87 patients had been treated and 62 surgeries were pending.

Kaleer. Kaleer was an outsider at age 15. He had endured taunts from classmates for at least 5 years prior to his high school years, and he began to doubt himself because of a lymphatic condition that had swelled his lower lip to 2½ times the normal size. In December 1998, he tearfully told his mother that he was tired of looking different, and he dropped out of high school. His mother found out that surgery to fix Kaleer's problem would cost $5,000 and that the insurance company was not willing to pay for what it considered a "cosmetic procedure." Family members had read in the newspaper about the Operation Smile's World Journey of Hope '99 and drove Kaleer and his mother to a screening clinic in New Brunswick, New Jersey. When he was selected for surgery, his mother told Operation Smile: "I told him one day there would be hope, and today's that day." The surgery was his Christmas present; Kaleer's gift to Operation Smile volunteers was his return to high school.

Marcia. Marcia was 10 years old when she was scheduled for surgery at a local clinic to remove an epidermal nevus from her neck. On the day of the surgery, she learned that her insurance company would not cover this procedure. Within a year, she learned of an Operation Smile screening in Washington, DC, and was overjoyed to know she was approved for surgery in January 1999. Before her operation, she had been very self-conscious and had tried to hide her mole by lowering her head to her chest.

Marcia is a different person now—full of energy—and she and her mother speak on behalf of Operation Smile, raising awareness so that other children can also have a new outlook on life.

Around the World

The World Journey of Hope '99 arrived for the first time in Quito, Ecuador, in February of that year. More than 400 potential patients were screened during the first 2 days. Families traveling from long distances were provided with bus transportation and shelters during their stay in Quito.

Juan. Before Juan was born, his mother, Miriam, had never seen a child with a cleft lip. Miriam's family treated her differently because of Juan's appearance, and Miriam knew she needed to seek help. She brought Juan to a doctor in her hometown of Santo Domingo who recommended that she take Juan to the Operation Smile doctors. Miriam, an unmarried mother of two children, didn't have the money to make the trip to Quito. She was told about the buses arranged for potential patients, and she made sure she and Juan were aboard. Juan was selected for surgery, and Miriam was overjoyed that her son would not only look "normal" but that he would no longer have difficulty in eating and drinking.

> *Because of the nature of this type of surgery, some U.S. insurance companies will not cover the cost and, in many cases, no insurance coverage has been provided for the patient through the parent's employment.*

Jesus. Jesus, a baby suffering from a bilateral cleft lip, traveled with his family a difficult 10 hours by bus from Colombia to Quito. The family had heard about Operation Smile through a friend of a neighbor who was studying medicine in Quito. Jesus' parents decided that the trip to Quito was worthwhile if there was a possibility that they could get help for their son. Before the team of doctors and medical volunteers arrived, the local Operation Smile chapter, Operacion Sonrisa Ecuador, began making arrangements for transportation and even provided a special bottle to make it easier for the baby to eat. Just 1 day before his 6-month birthday, Jesus was given the gift of hope through reconstructive surgery. Rosa Witt de Mahuad, the mother of Ecuador's president, Jamil Mahuad, carried Jesus to his mother and father following surgery.

Ibran. In mid-March, the World Journey of Hope '99 arrived in Bucharest, Romania. The volunteer mission team screened 223 potential patients. During an exhausting week of surgery, 126 procedures were performed on 83 patients, many of whom suffered from horrible burns and burn contractures.

One patient, Ibran, was brought to the hospital by her caretakers from the orphanage where she lives, 400 kilometers from Bucharest. Then 14 months old, Ibran was not considered very adoptable because of a bilateral cleft lip and palate. Her biological parents had abandoned her to the orphanage at her birth because of her deformity. Although Ibran was small in stature, she was in good health and was readily accepted for surgery. The hospital staff reported that she never cried, even though she was in the company of strangers. In fact, she was open to anyone who would hold her. Following her successful surgery, she went back to the orphanage with a new smile to await an adoptive family.

Xiaoma. In April [1999], the Operation Smile team arrived in China and encountered a young boy with a remarkable story. On a wintry day, a baby boy was abandoned on a street next to a factory simply because he had been born with a cleft lip, a facial deformity easily repaired through a 45-minute surgery. Chen Yongtai found the baby and took him home, although his wife refused to have anything to do with the child. They already had three sons to support on a combined income of $87 a month from his job as a self-employed blacksmith and her job at a local factory. But the 63-year-old man could not turn his back on the infant. He named him Xiaoma and was his sole caretaker for 1 year. The baby's sweetness and intelligence soon drew Mrs. Yongtai into caring for him as well.

In 1998, Mr. Yongtai heard that Operation Smile was coming to Nanjing. He and Xiaoma traveled for 10 hours by bus to the screening, but his son was not selected for surgery at that time. In 1999, they made the 10-hour journey once more, and this time Xiaoma was chosen to have his cleft lip repaired.

The Operation Smile team was mesmerized by the relationship between this father and son. They stood by and quietly watched the tears that continually ran down Mr. Yongtai's cheeks as he caressed Xiaoma's head and wiped the blood away from his son's nose and mouth. Once the anesthesia wore off and Xiaoma could sit up to look at himself in the mirror, the 8-year-old repeatedly traced his finger over the perfect red lips of the doll he was holding and stared back at his new reflection in the mirror. Soon everyone was crying.

Xiaoma's story reminds us that each child deserves a life of dignity and hope, one that is free from isolation, abandonment, and shame. This simple truth is why 3,000 Operation Smile volunteers joined together in 1999 for 9 weeks in 18 countries to change the lives of 5,000 children and their families. This simple truth made the largest-ever surgical mission a reality. This was a world journey of hope!

Increasing Numbers of American Men Are Getting Cosmetic Surgery

Bill Troy

Bill Troy is a contributing writer for Cosmetic Surgery Times, *a monthly newsmagazine that provides patients and doctors with information about cosmetic surgery.*

Statistics show that an increasing number of men in the United States are receiving cosmetic surgery. While this trend is most pronounced on the East and West coasts, it is also visible in the Midwest, where cosmetic surgeons are seeing more and more male patients in their offices. Multiple factors are causing the increase in this surgery. One is vanity and the ease with which men can now correct genetic imperfections through surgery. Another reason is the desire of aging baby boomers to gain an advantage in competitive job markets. Television has also played a major role in making cosmetic surgery more socially acceptable for men. According to research on the subject, the soaring number of male surgery patients is not just a U.S. phenomenon; plastic surgery for men is growing in popularity around the world.

A few years ago, male patients were something of a rarity in a plastic surgeon's waiting room. More likely than not, they didn't even want anyone to know they'd been there.

But figures just released [in 2004] by the American Society for Aesthetic Plastic Surgery (ASAPS) show that not only are American men now finding plenty of male company in the doctor's office, it may not trouble them in the least to talk about their treatment.

American men [are] now finding plenty of male company in the [plastic surgeon's] office.

According to ASAPS, 1.1 million American men underwent cosmetic surgery procedures during 2003. By contrast, ASAPS reports that in 1997, only 287,000 American men were cosmetic patients. That's a six year growth of 269 percent, or an average increase of about 45 percent per year. That same study showed that 74 percent of the men interviewed said they wouldn't be embarrassed if others knew they'd had cosmetic surgery.

From these statistics, one might be easily persuaded that male patients are primarily responsible for the recent growth of U.S. cosmetic surgery. Not really, says ASAPS. During that same six-year span, the number of female patients, according to their studies, soared from 1.8 million in 1997 to 7.2 million in 2003, a six-year gain of 289 percent. While the patient numbers of both genders have increased dramatically, the comparative gender percentages have, in fact, stayed roughly the same through the years, at about 87 percent female and 13 percent male. Nothing in the available statistics, an ASAPS spokesperson said, indicates that those percentages are likely to change much in the near future.

Vanity and Insecurity as Driving Forces

One can assume that vanity is an important driving force in the increase of male cosmetic surgery patients. Illinois surgeon Dr. Mark Zukowski said his male clients are not only younger than they used to be, but appear to be less compelled to accept genetic quirks that affect their appearance, such as misshaped noses or protruding ears. "I know it sounds a far-fetched," Dr. Zukowski said, "but I honestly believe the events of 9/11[1] have

1. the terrorist attacks of September 11, 2001

influenced the thinking of a lot of young people. Like a young man said to me the other day, 'Why should I put up with genetic imperfection until I'm 50? I might not be here then.'"

But less esoteric reasons for male patient growth are also coming into play. Baby boomers are now experiencing the pains and wrinkles of their mid-50s, and along with those comes the threat of job loss or job insecurity in an intensely competitive global job market. In the opinion of many human resource executives, gray hair and crow's feet now represent a job seeker's vulnerability, rather than the wisdom and experience they might once have conveyed. In a recent Internet article, under the imprint Starbanner.com, Dr. Sherrell Aston, a well-known New York plastic surgeon, reportedly said that 17 percent of his patients undergoing eyelid surgery and 11 percent of those choosing facelifts are now male, double the percentage of 10 years ago. In that same article, Dr. Diana Bihova, a New York dermatologist, is reported as saying that 40 percent of her cosmetic patients are now men seeking Botox, collagen, chemical peels and other skin treatments.

The "Coastal" Theory

"I wouldn't dispute any of that," said Dr. Randall Yetman in Cleveland, "but I'd have to add that at the present time, I think the increase in male patients is more governed by cultural, even geographical, considerations. Maybe I can define it as 'coastal.' Everything I hear indicates that the growth of male patient rosters is exploding on both the East and West coasts. But I don't believe it's come to the Midwest yet. It will. Trends in this country tend to begin on the coasts and then drift inland. But I haven't seen it yet here. About 20 percent of my patients are male, but that's been true for a number of years."

> *Vanity is an important driving force in the increase of male cosmetic surgery patients.*

Dr. Zukowski's patient ratios are similar. "About 20 percent are men, and have been right along. Midwestern attitudes are simply more conservative. It takes more time to make changes. But I can say that the biggest growth in my practice is coming from younger people, both male and female, in the 24-to-35 group. Also, I think the increased availability of treatment on an outpatient basis is also an important contributor. Ninety-six percent of my treatment work is now done in the office."

> *Television is . . . fast becoming a powerful new ally in promoting cosmetic surgery and treatment, and making it more socially acceptable.*

Dr. Tina Alster of Washington, D.C., has a rapid-fire answer when asked if she's treating more men patients. "Absolutely," she said. "It used to be that men represented less than 5 percent of my patients. Now it's in excess of 10 percent and growing, particularly with the onset of more non-invasive skin treatment procedures. But I will say this," she added, "most of the men showing up in my office are there because their female partners told them to."

Dr. Alster readily supports the "coastal" theory advanced by Drs. Yetman and Zukowski, but she gives it a practical twist. "You've got to remember that most of our coastal cities are in more temperate climates. People don't wear as much clothing. So more of their bodies are seen, and they're sensitive to the fact."

The Influence of Television

Another factor she considers in measuring overall cosmetic surgery increases: "There are more and more references on TV sitcoms to people undergoing cosmetic surgery. Not only does that attract new patients, but it appeals to a younger audience."

With its unique ability to visually dramatize the "before" and "after" aspects of cosmetic surgery, television is indeed fast becoming a powerful new ally in promoting cosmetic surgery and treatment, and making it more socially acceptable. Virtually all of the broadcast networks, along with their local affiliates, as well as the cable news outlets now have full-time health reporters. They are often people with medical degrees or training.

As a March 15 [2004] news segment on CNN [Cable News Network] demonstrated, cosmetic surgery is a particularly appropriate subject for audience interaction, the new staple of television news. E-mail questions poured in on the cost, safety and propriety of undergoing plastic surgery. In the space of one hour, Dr. Julius Few, a plastic surgeon in Chicago, elicited several hundred e-mail queries on subjects such as liposuction, nose reshaping, facelifting and various other treatments and procedures. Will it be safe? What will it cost? How quickly will I recover? For those promoting the growth of cosmetic surgery, it had to be a dream come true.

A Worldwide Trend

It's readily apparent that the increased number of male cosmetic surgery patients isn't just a U.S. phenomenon. On Feb. 23, 2003, the *New York Times* ran an article on plastic surgery among the men of Bogota, Colombia. That article, which appeared on the *Times'* Web page, reported that men now account for 30 percent of cosmetic surgeries in Bogota, up from 10 percent just five years ago. The article further states that these figures "are a reflection of trends across Brazil, Argentina and the rest of Latin America."

While it wasn't really its purpose, the ASAPS growth figures also seem to be saying that cosmetic surgery may be one of the fastest-growing professions in the civilized world.

3

Thousands of Asians Are Turning to Cosmetic Surgery

Lisa Takeuchi Cullen

Lisa Takeuchi Cullen is a staff writer for TimeAsia *magazine.*

In the past, cosmetic surgery was not nearly as popular in Asia as it was in Western countries, in part because Asians had less discretionary income than Westerners and because there were fewer qualified surgeons. However, more women and men are opting for cosmetic procedures in Asia and today the industry is beginning to boom. The number of surgeries in Korea, Japan, and Taiwan is increasing every year. The most popular surgeries are for wider eyes, longer noses, and fuller breasts, all of which are features not typical of Asians. Surgeons are even developing techniques to change the shape of the typically muscular calves of Asians. In Asian countries where virginity is highly prized, hymen reconstruction is popular. Millions of Asians are buying into the idea that they need to look young and to "improve" their features.

At 18, Saeko Kimura was a shy, sleepy-eyed university student. Until she discovered a secret weapon: if she applied a strip of glue to her eyelids, her eyes became wider, rounder, prettier. "Men noticed me," she says. "I became outgoing. Suddenly, I had a life." Her new looks also landed her part-time work as a hostess in an upmarket bar, where she gets top dollar on a pay scale determined by beauty.

But Kimura lived in fear of discovery, rushing off to the bathroom several times a day to reapply the glue and never daring to visit the beach. And so, at 21, she finds herself in a doctor's office in a Tokyo high-rise, lying on an operating table with her fists nervously clenched. Plastic surgeon Katsuya Takasu breezes in wielding a cartoonishly enormous needle. "This will hurt a little," he says cheerfully. Once the anesthetic is administered, Takasu brandishes another hooked needle and threads it through Kimura's upper eyelids, creating a permanent crease. He then injects a filler fluid called hyaluronic acid into her nose and chin and pinches them into shape. Takasu inspects his handiwork. "The swelling will go down in a few days," he says. "But even if you went out tonight in Roppongi, you'd be a hit." A nurse hands Kimura a mirror. Though red and puffy, she now has the face she's always dreamed of: big, round eyes, a tall nose, a defined chin. The entire procedure took less than 10 minutes. But Kimura collapses with an ice pack on her face and moans, "Oh, the pain."

What we won't do for beauty. Around Asia, women—and increasingly, men—are nipping and tucking, sucking and suturing, injecting and implanting, all in the quest for better looks. In the past, Asia had lagged behind the West in catching the plastic surgery wave, held back by cultural hang-ups, arrested medical skills and a poorer consumer base. But cosmetic surgery is now booming throughout Asia like never before. In Taiwan, a million procedures were performed last year, double the number from five years ago. In Korea, surgeons estimate that at least one in 10 adults have received some form of surgical upgrade and even tots have their eyelids done. The government of Thailand has taken to hawking plastic surgery tours. In Japan, non-invasive procedures dubbed "petite surgery" have set off such a rage that top clinics are raking in $100 million a year.

Elsewhere in Asia, this explosion of personal re-engineering is harder to document, because for every skilled and legitimate surgeon there seethes a swarm of shady pretenders. Indonesia, for instance, boasts only 43 licensed plastic surgeons for a population of about 230 million; yet an estimated 400 illicit procedures are performed each week in the capital alone. In Shenzhen, the Chinese boomtown, thousands of unlicensed "beauty-science centers" lure hordes of upwardly mobile patients, looking to buy a new pair of eyes or a new nose as the perfect accessory to their new cars and new clothes.

The results are often disastrous. In China alone, over 200,000 lawsuits were filed in the past decade against cosmetic surgery practitioners, according to the *China Quality Daily*, an official consumer protection newspaper. The dangers are greatest in places like Shenzhen that specialize in cut-price procedures. "Any Tom, Dick or Harry with a piece of paper—genuine or not—can practice over there," says Dr. Philip Hsieh, a Hong Kong–based plastic surgeon. "They use things that have not been approved, just for a quick buck. And people in China don't know that they're subjecting themselves to this kind of risk."

Of course, Asians have always suffered for beauty. Consider the ancient practice of foot binding in China, or the stacked, brass coils used to distend the necks of Karen women. In fact, some of the earliest records of reconstructive plastic surgery come from sixth century India: the Hindu medical chronicle *Susruta Samhita* describes how noses were recreated after being chopped off as punishment for adultery.

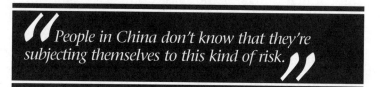
People in China don't know that they're subjecting themselves to this kind of risk.

The culturally loaded issue today is the number of Asians looking to remake themselves to look more Caucasian. It's a charge many deny, although few would argue that under the relentless bombardment of Hollywood, satellite TV, and Madison Avenue, Asia's aesthetic ideal has changed drastically. "Beauty, after all, is evolutionary," says Harvard psychology professor Nancy Etcoff, who is the author of *Survival of the Prettiest: The Science of Beauty*—not coincidentally a best seller in Japan, Korea, Hong Kong and China. Asians are increasingly asking their surgeons for wider eyes, longer noses and fuller breasts—features not typical of the race. To accommodate such demands, surgeons in the region have had to invent unique techniques. The No. 1 procedure by far in Asia is a form of blepharoplasty, in which a crease is created above the eye by scalpel or by needle and thread; in the U.S., blepharoplasty also ranks near the top, but involves removing bags and fat around the eyes. Likewise, Westerners use botox, or botulinum toxin, to diminish wrinkles—while in Korea, Japan and Taiwan, botox is injected into wide cheeks so the muscle will atrophy and the cheeks will shrink. Just as Asian faces require unique procedures, their bodies demand innovative operations to achieve the leggy, skinny, busty Western ideal that has become increasingly universal. Dr. Suh In Seock, a surgeon in Seoul, has struggled to find the best way to fix an affliction the Koreans call *muu-dari* and the Japanese call *daikon-ashi*: radish-shaped calves. Liposuction, so effective on the legs of plump Westerners, doesn't work on Asians since muscle, not fat, accounts for the bulk. Suh says earlier attempts to carve the muscle were painful and made walking difficult. "Finally, I discovered that by severing a nerve behind the knee, the muscle would atrophy," says Suh, "thereby reducing its size up to 40%." Suh has performed over 600 of the operations since 1996. He disappears for a minute and returns with a bottle of fluid containing what looks like chopped up bits of ramen noodles. He has preserved his patients' excised nerves in alcohol. "And that's just since November," he says proudly.

The cultural quirks of the plastic surgery business in Asia also extend to sexuality. In China, Korea and Indonesia, where virginity is highly prized, young women go in for hymen reconstruction in time for their wedding night. In Japan, Indonesia and Korea, men ask for penis-enlargement procedures, in part to avoid shame when bathing en masse. In Thailand, with its sizable population of so-called "lady boys," a thriving industry has sprung up to provide male-to-female sex-change operations.

Traditionally, most Asians going under the scalpel were women. But a mutant strain of male vanity has turned into a virtual epidemic. "Men are uptight about seeming too vain," says Dr. Takasu after completing the procedure on Kimura. "But it's true that when you look old, you're treated that way." He clicks his computer mouse and a close-up of a saggy-faced, dour man appears on a flat, wall-mounted monitor. "That's me four years ago," he says with a satisfied chortle. "Lifts," he explains, batting his eyes and stroking his jaw. "Chemical peel," he says, sweeping a hand across his face. "Plugs," he adds, tilting his brown-dyed hair forward. "I had a colleague insert a golden wire in my chin to prevent sagging." Takasu, who looks a decade younger than his 57 years, uses his own face as an advertisement prop for his trade, and it glows like a large peach.

Today, all beauty requires is cash—and Asians are blowing it on surgery at an unprecedented rate. "People want to look more beautiful as a way to show off their newfound wealth," explains Dr. He Xiaoming of the Peking Medical Union College's Plastic Surgery Hospital. Dr. Jean Lin, a plastic surgeon in Taipei, adds: "When the market goes up, I get more patients. When it drops, so do my appointments." On the other hand, a tight labor market also forces workers to compete by trying to look more attractive. In Japan, salarymen buzz about "recruit seikei"—cosmetic surgery for the sake of landing a job. The owner of a "beauty center" in Shenzen's Jiulong City Mall observes, "China has too many people. How do you make yourself stand out from 1.3 billion? Imagine your boss sees two people of similar ability. He will definitely pick the person with the better appearance."

"Of course, Asians have always suffered for beauty."

In China, surgically enhanced beauty is both a way to display wealth and a tool with which to attain it. Audis of the rich and well connected cram the parking lot of the high-tech Shenzhen Fuhua Plastic & Aesthetic Hospital, where the operating rooms look like a Star Trek set. The surgery center at Northwest University in Xi'an, a city in western China, targets a different demographic, handing out promotional flyers that offer procedures including hymen reconstruction at a 50% discount for students—"in order to make you tops in both your academic achievements and your looks!"

In recession-plagued Thailand, even the government has recognized the money-making potential of plastic surgery. The Tourism Authority of Thailand helps promote institutions like the Bumrungrad Hospital to foreigners, who make up one-third of its patients. "We're a hot commodity," says Ruben Toral, the hospital's director of international programs. Located on a traffic-clogged street in Bangkok, the 12-story, $90 million hospital is like a five-star, round-the-clock plastic surgery factory. There's a Starbucks in the lobby, high-speed Internet connection for the patients and room service offering halal and kosher meals.

In the mid-'70s, Thailand had only 10 plastic surgeons, so locals tended to go abroad to Japan or Singapore for cosmetic help. Today, the tide has reversed, and Thailand has become a surgical hub. "No country can compete with Thailand," says Dr. Preecha Tiewtranon, a surgeon specializing in sex reassignment at Bangkok's Preecha Aesthetic Institute, where 80% of the clientele is foreign. Much of the appeal is price: Preecha, who performed 300 operations last year, charges only $6,000 for a sex change, compared to $25,000 in the West. Price, too, is what attracts foreign patients—mainly from Japan, Taiwan and Hong Kong—to Apkujong, a section of Seoul with over 400 surgery clinics. Here, on a busy avenue nicknamed "Plastic Surgery Street," Park Chan Hoon pulls up in his sedan and leads three female passengers into a softly lit lobby decked out in black leather and chrome. A few years ago, the 38-year-old engineering Ph.D. quit a research job to start a travel agency offering plastic surgery tours for the Japanese. Packages include airfare, hotel, sightseeing and, say, a boob job—all for the cost of the procedure alone back home.

Park jokes in fluent Japanese with Satsuki Takemoto, who has traveled to Seoul for shopping and liposuction. The 34-year-old homemaker from Hiroshima pulls out a snapshot of a stunning woman in a red kimono. "That's me 10 years ago," she says. She once weighed 40 kilos; today, after having two children, she's 75 kilos. "My husband says he doesn't care," rasps Takemoto, exhaling cigarette smoke, "but when the kids are mad at me they'll sometimes yell, 'buta'"—pig. Over the years, Takemoto has tried prescription diets, spa treatments, specially-designed slimming underwear—all of which were expensive and none of which worked. Surgery, especially at a decent price, seemed the smart solution. "We told the kids, 'Mommy's in Korea getting her fat sucked out because we don't want her to drop dead from heart failure,'" she says. She takes another drag on her cigarette. "Yeah, they're a little scared."

Kawinna Suwanpradeep, an actress known throughout Thailand for her roles in TV soap operas, wasn't scared. Plastic surgery is no big deal in her line of work, and Suwanpradeep, 32, was less concerned about medical risks than the risk of losing work due to her hefty thighs. When Yanhee Hospital, a Bangkok plastic surgery center, offered her free liposuction in return for a public endorsement, she jumped at the chance. "I figured the doctors were internationally trained, and a lot of stars went there," she says. "I hadn't heard that a lot of things had gone wrong."

She was told she would be able to go home the same day as

the operation, "but I had to stay three days," says Suwanpradeep. "I couldn't walk because of the pain and weakness." After the bandages were removed, she noticed wavy patches and scars. The doctor told her they would disappear in a few months, but when they still hadn't healed a year later, she demanded an explanation. "Then his whole tone changed and he said it wouldn't heal—that I would have to have another operation."

Instead, Suwanpradeep went to court: "I can't wear swimsuits. I can't do fashion shoots. And I can't play any sexy characters on television, because at some point they might have to show their legs." The hospital denies responsibility (and declined to comment for this article, citing the pending court case). Disgusted with her courthouse experience, Suwanpradeep is studying for a law degree. "Now," she says, "I'm the poster girl for plastic surgery disaster."

> ❝ Liposuction, so effective on the legs of plump Westerners, doesn't work on Asians since muscle, not fat, accounts for the bulk. ❞

That's a poster that should be plastered around countless back lanes offering cut-rate beauty—especially in Thailand, Indonesia and China, where outdated laws offer scant protection against crooks and incompetents. In Indonesia, a thriving underground of beauty parlors and door-to-door salesmen cash in on perhaps the most rampant and dangerous procedure available in Asia: silicone injections, which are strictly regulated in the U.S. In Asia, silicone is still hawked to plump up noses, breasts and even sex organs like the labia or penis. It works at first, but liquid silicone can't escape the laws of gravity, resulting eventually in an unsightly droop. It can also cause swelling, tissue decay, and—if it enters the bloodstream—death. Transsexuals are often both perpetrators and victims. Two years ago, a transsexual in East Java died after injecting silicone into her breasts. What's more, the injectable silicone typically used among transsexuals is industrial grade—much cheaper and more toxic than medical-grade silicone. "To make even more money," adds Dede Oetomo, a Surabaya-based anthropologist and gay activist, "they heat the substance and mix it with cod-liver oil, lard or frying oil."

Saleha, now 33, received her first silicone injection in 1995 from a fellow transsexual who owned a beauty parlor in Surabaya. Tall, slender and dressed in a tight, white top and matching miniskirt, Saleha would be attractive if not for her ruined nose and chin. After her first cosmetic injection, she wound up with a nose "like Bozo the clown's," she says. So she visited another beautician who pinched and tweaked her nose into shape, then treated her with more injections than Saleha can now count. "I was totally broke after a while," says Saleha, who at the time sold noodles and moonlighted as a prostitute. Gradually, as the silicone shifted, her whole face began to sag and her chin withered. When she speaks, her large hands flutter constantly to her face to perform a furtive, futile massage. Part of the problem is that it's much harder to exact legal retribution in Asia than in the West, where medical malpractice suits often yield enormous settlements. Most Asian lawyers avoid malpractice cases, since so few result in victory and financial payoff. Above all, though, it's the bargain-hunting instinct that leads patients astray, tempting them to use unqualified cosmetic practitioners. "At the end of the day, the government will have to make a decision on whether to restrict surgery to specialists," says Dr. Woffles Wu, a plastic surgeon at the Camden Medical Center in Singapore. "This is a time bomb waiting to go off."

How do you make yourself stand out from 1.3 billion?

It may seem reckless to undergo medically unnecessary operations that could disfigure or even kill you. But who's to say that good looks aren't worth the risk? "The Japanese have a saying: 'It's not the face, it's the heart,'" says television producer Koji Kaneda. "But when I asked around, everyone acknowledged appearances count—often more than anything." With that in mind, Kaneda dreamed up a show called *Beauty Colosseum* that launched last fall. Each week, women pour forth tales of woe, and a panel of beauty experts offers makeover advice. The most desperate cases are referred to the show's "miracle doctor of beauty," Toshiya Handa, a surgeon at the Otsuka Academy of Cosmetic & Plastic Surgery, a chain of 13 clinics across Japan. The regular appearance of tanned, telegenic Handa on *Beauty Colosseum* has inspired a flood of young TV viewers to sign up for surgery at Otsuka. In 2001, 64% of the patients there were in their teens or 20s.

> **❝***Imagine your boss sees two people of similar ability. He will definitely pick the person with the better appearance.***❞**

One of the program's most memorable guests was Yumi Sakaguchi, a 26-year-old from Osaka. Even today, her lips tremble as she recounts her life. Born with droopy eyes, a receding chin and prominent buckteeth, Sakaguchi endured merciless teasing in her youth. Classmates even drew caricatures of her on the chalkboard. "I always walked with my face to the ground," she says. After high school, when her diabetic father racked up big medical bills, Sakaguchi sought work as a bar hostess to pay off the family debt. "They turned me away flat, saying, 'You'd make the customers sick,'" she recalls. "It was then I realized I had only my body to sell." Sakaguchi found work at a brothel, but many customers rejected her because of her looks. "I was at rock bottom," she says, softly. "I kept thinking, something will work out, somehow. My life depended on it."

Last October, Sakaguchi appeared on *Beauty Colosseum* and won free dental, eye and chin surgery that would otherwise have cost over $30,000. She quit the skin trade, landed a high-paying hostess job, and plans to study psychology. But nearly a year after her surgical windfall, Sakaguchi sounds circumspect, as if the enormity of the change has come to weigh on her. Though open about her surgery and her past, she was hurt when a recent boyfriend told her he would not have dated her before her surgical alteration. "I always wanted to believe people were ultimately judged by what was inside," she muses, her gaze hesitant and sad. "But I knew from my personal experience that this wasn't true. It's always the pretty girls who win the good things in life."

Alvin Goh, a slight, impeccably dressed stylist and creative director of a soon-to-be-launched lifestyle magazine in Singapore, understands better than most our tendency to judge a book by its cover. So, a year and a half ago, Goh, now 24, de-

28

cided to get an eye job. "We live in a cruel society where everything is based on first impressions," he says. "If you look in the mirror and don't feel good about what you see, it won't help you in your life, in your work or in your relationships."

All of Asia is ruled by a youth culture.

Much more so than women, men cite their careers as the driving reason to go under the knife. Taiwanese comedian Tsai Tou was once known as the ugliest man in show business. While his face helped win him laughs, he felt it limited his chances of hosting a talk show: so he too had surgery two years ago, adding folds to his eyelids, getting his eye bags removed, having his nose heightened and his wrinkles flattened with botox. A face free of bags and wrinkles, Tsai explains, captures the "*trustworthy*" look that TV viewers prefer. Dr. Kenneth Hui, a plastic surgeon in Hong Kong, remarks: "It can be a matter of necessity, not vanity."

Necessity drove Ching Wei to plastic surgery. Desperate for work, the struggling Taiwanese entertainer took a TV role in 1997 that required him to escape chains and a wooden box as it was set on fire. Instead, he found himself trapped. Covered with third-degree burns, Ching saw his career evaporate and attempted suicide. Five years and $60,000 worth of surgery later, Ching, now 37, is an award-winning media personality and owner of his own communications company. "It's a miracle," he says. "Everything you see about me is the work of plastic surgery—my facial skin, implanted hair, and restored retina."

Some people find tragedy in the plastic surgery clinic. Others, like Sakaguchi and Ching, are reborn. Most are somehow looking to achieve that most elusive of goals: to halt the march of time. "All of Asia is ruled by a youth culture," says Hiromi Yamamoto, a Tokyo hair and makeup artist who has written extensively about plastic surgery. "We may respect the old, but it's the young who play the lead roles. So it's no surprise that the old want to look young, and the young want to look fabulous."

In a plush cabaret in the Akasaka entertainment district of Tokyo, a slender woman in a slinky, red dress croons *Amazing Grace*. Despite her rich voice and charming stage presence, Teri Hirayama is, at 36, pushing the upper limits of the business. So, over the course of six months, she has had her baggy eyelids lifted, her nose and chin shaped, and her wrinkles smoothed away. Now the politicians and foreign executives who frequent the joint ply Hirayama with requests.

"I'm the one who urged her to get it done," boasts cabaret owner Kirisa Matsui, herself a gorgeous specimen of 60. "I don't hire homely girls. These are difficult times, you know, and I've got a business to run."

Whether for vanity, ego or cold hard cash, we all want to look better, younger, more fabulous. Think of all the clichés about beauty: that it is in the eye of the beholder, that it slayed the beast and, of course, that it is only skin deep. Teri Hirayama and millions more throughout the region seem to be buying into that last conceit as they go under the knife in the quest for an aesthetic beauty as malleable as silicone in a surgeon's hand.

4

Smooth Operations

Allison Samuels

Allison Samuels is a correspondent in Newsweek's *Los Angeles bureau. She covers sports and entertainment, and won the 1997 National Association of Black Journalists Award for* Newsweek's *March 17, 1997, cover story "Black Like Who?" She is a member of the National Association of Black Journalists, the Big Sisters of America, and the UCLA black studies department's board of directors.*

African Americans have long held cultural taboos against cosmetic surgery. Even black celebrities, whose looks are critical to their jobs, have hesitated to alter their appearance through surgical means. The African American community has traditionally rejected cosmetic surgery, particularly procedures to change wide noses and to promote weight loss, because altering those features was seen as an insult to their culture and ancestors. African Americans also have skin that scars easily, which has been a deterrent to elective surgery. However, today more and more African Americans are opting for cosmetic surgery. By 2003 nearly 5 percent of cosmetic surgery procedures were performed on African Americans. They have become the biggest consumers of beauty products in the United States, spending at least $20 billion a year. The increase of surgeries on black patients is an extension of the trend.

Long before Janet Jackson revealed a little too much of her body, Tanisha Rollins was obsessed with having one just like it. After watching the singer strut in a 1993 video, Rollins embarked on a quest for washboard abs. For the next decade she stuck to a rigorous regimen. But her abs pretty much stayed the same. Then a friend skipped all the hard work and got a tummy

30

tuck. "I was just like, 'What magazines have you been reading?!'" says Rollins, 29, an administrative assistant in Dayton, Ohio. She thought nipping and tucking was only for "rich white people and Michael Jackson," not African-American women like her, making $30,000 a year.

[In 2003] Rollins shelled out $5,000 for a tummy tuck of her own, joining the small but growing ranks of African-Americans opting for cosmetic surgery. The number of blacks seeking facial or reconstructive surgery more than tripled between 1997 and 2002, reflecting both the growing affluence of African-Americans and the subtle easing of some long-held cultural taboos against such procedures. Except for the Jacksons (or perhaps because of them), even black celebrities, whose looks are essential to their livelihood, have been loath to go under the knife. "I was just so worried about looking crazy or looking like Jennifer Grey, who no one recognized after she had her nose job," says one 40-year-old black actress, who decided last year to have her nose and breasts done after being inspired by singer Patti LaBelle. (Though LaBelle, 60, talks about her nose job, the actress requested anonymity.)

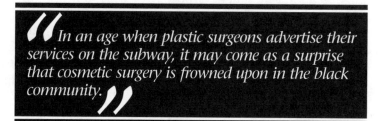

In an age when plastic surgeons advertise their services on the subway, it may come as a surprise that cosmetic surgery is frowned upon in the black community.

In an age when plastic surgeons advertise their services on the subway, it may come as a surprise that cosmetic surgery is frowned upon in the black community. "People want to look good," says Dr. Karen Low, who is African-American and a plastic surgeon in Greensboro, N.C., "but they also want to avoid any criticism that might come from the community, which has for years supported larger frames, wider noses and not-so-perfect features. Changing those things is sometimes seen as an insult to our ancestors and to the culture." Rollins experienced that backlash when she told her family she was having a tummy tuck. Not only did they think it was risky and expensive, they couldn't understand why she wanted to tinker with "God's work." "It's hard telling your mother that you don't want to look like her when you're 50," Rollins says. "I think my mother resented that and felt hurt, but I had to be honest."

There's a lot more at work here than simple vanity. "I think African-American women have finally just decided that it's time to love ourselves," says *Essence* magazine beauty editor Miki Taylor. African-Americans have become the biggest consumers of beauty products in the United States, spending at least $20 billion a year, as companies like L'Oreal, which opened its Institute for Ethnic Hair and Skin Research in 2003, are well aware. The increase in plastic surgery is in many ways an extension of that trend.

Blacks accounted for nearly 5 percent of the 8.7 million cosmetic-surgery procedures done last year. As the numbers have grown, doctors have had to adapt to their clientele. For starters, black women and white women tend to want to tune up different areas of their bodies. While the nose is Job No. 1 for whites, black women's top request is the tummy tuck. Breast enhancement? More black women want reductions. "Let's be clear that I did it for my health," says rapper-actress Queen Latifah, who went from a double-E bra cup to a D. Face-lifts are not as popular as they are among white women, a testament, perhaps, to a long-held belief in the African-American community: "Black don't crack."

But black skin does scar, much more easily than white skin, and that has been a big deterrent to African-Americans considering elective surgery. Doctors try to be as minimally invasive as possible, using lasers and making smaller incisions, hiding scars in inconspicuous places, and using electron-beam radiation to diminish the appearance of scars. Dermatologist Marcia Glenn, who opened Odyssey Medispa in Marina del Rey, Calif., with an eye toward African-American women like herself, encourages patients to try less-invasive procedures like Botox before choosing surgery.

Like many women who have cosmetic surgery, Patti LaBelle was hoping to cut away at her insecurities in the process. Looking at childhood pictures, "I realized I wasn't a very good-looking girl," says the singer, who was teased mercilessly about her broad nose. "I didn't like the way that made me feel." As middle age sank in, she hoped surgery would make her feel better about herself. Rather than go for a button nose, LaBelle was sensitive about keeping her features looking African-American. "Nothing drastic, just enough to make me feel and look as good as I could," she says. "If, in a few years, I want to get some more work done on my chin or my neck, I will."

5

The Desire to Look Young Is the Main Reason People Seek Cosmetic Surgery

Courtney Lomax

Courtney Lomax is a writer for the Express-Times.

Society's pressures to look young, especially those that are placed on women, have caused an increase in the number of cosmetic surgery procedures that are performed. Most patients feel the desire to look younger and want their faces to have a fresh, rejuvenated look. However, some patients want surgery for reasons that are completely inappropriate, such as to further their career or to appear more desirable to a boyfriend or husband. Surgeons should screen their patients to determine their motives. Surgeons should also attempt to determine if the patients fully understand the potential risks and outcomes of cosmetic surgery. Cosmetic procedures are continually evolving, and in the future, it may even be possible for patients to get face transplants.

Elective cosmetic surgery is in.

But what draws people to these trendy surgeries?

"Psychologically, it makes you feel good to look younger," says Dr. Manny Iyer of Lehigh Plastic Surgery Center in Bethlehem [Pennsylvania]. "People don't want to have a tired look."

However, some critics wonder about the ethics of a society

that emphasizes youthful appearance.

Appearances inevitably change with age, says Elizabeth Meade, chairwoman of the humanities department and associate professor of philosophy at Cedar Crest College in Allentown.

The requirements for "ageless beauty" are not the same for men and women.

For example, a news anchorwoman may receive plastic surgery to look younger and keep her job. But that isn't expected of men, Meade says.

It's common for individuals, mostly women, to desire a facial procedure that will make them look younger. A younger-looking face has fewer wrinkles and a clear jaw line without jowls, Iyer says.

People get face lifts because they want a rejuvenated look, says Dr. Robert Kevitch of Aesthetic Surgery Associates in Allentown.

Because of gravity and lack of skin tension, the skin on the face falls and people begin to look older and tired. Hereditary factors may even contribute to an aged look, Kevitch says.

Face lifts generally last seven to 10 years and are most common among people ages 45 to 55.

The cost of a rejuvenated look often is not covered by health insurance companies, according to the American Society of Plastic Surgeons [ASPS] Web site.

Cosmetic Surgeries Are Increasing in Popularity

Common elective cosmetic procedures are eyelid lifts, face lifts and nose reshaping, Kevitch says. Iyer adds chin augmentation and forehead lifts to the list.

The average cost of these procedures is between $1,693 and $5,283, according to the ASPS. Chin augmentation is the least expensive procedure and face lifts the most expensive.

Despite the cost, elective cosmetic procedures are increasing in popularity.

Eyelid surgeries have increased 7 percent, face lifts 9 percent and nose reconstruction 1 percent. There were more than 8.7 million cosmetic procedures performed in 2003. This is a 33-percent increase from 2002, according the ASPS.

Ninety percent of people who have cosmetic surgery are female, Kevitch says.

"Although it is unfair, men can get away with having wrinkles on their face and still appear attractive in society," he says.

Instead of receiving the common female procedures of eyelid lifts, face lifts, nose jobs, chin implants, forehead lifts or brow lifts, men are more likely to have hair transplants.

However, both men and women want to look younger through plastic surgery, American Academy of Facial Plastic and Reconstructive Surgery [AAFPRS] surgeons report. Men are more likely to give work-related reasons for surgery while women want procedures to improve their self-esteem.

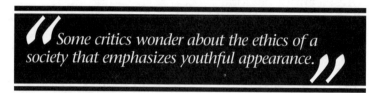

Some critics wonder about the ethics of a society that emphasizes youthful appearance.

"Feminists believe in a woman's right to complete autonomy over her body," Meade says. "This right includes elective cosmetic surgery."

At the same time, feminists recognize women generally receive cosmetic surgery to "conform to societal ideals of beauty" which can oppress women, she says.

"Women shouldn't have to live in a society of such narrow standards of beauty," Meade says. They can be "coerced by unattainable societal ideals of beauty."

Feminists have a right to educate people about the "risks of cosmetic surgery and the danger of mass conformity."

At the same time, it would be condescending to tell women they cannot have cosmetic surgery because they are conforming to societal ideals. Women should not be made to feel guilty or bad about their feeling toward elective cosmetic surgery, Meade says.

Motives for Surgery

Surgeons should follow whatever guidelines the profession provides when questioning the motives of a person seeking elective cosmetic surgery, she says.

Iyer says he always screens his patients' motives by evaluating their history, physical features and the desired procedure. If he feels it is necessary, he asks the patient to have a psychological screening to be sure the procedure is wanted for the right reasons.

Poor reasons to want facial surgery include wanting a work-related promotion or expecting a significant other to be more attracted to the patient after the surgery, Iyer says.

Kevitch agrees.

"If the patient thinks her husband or boyfriend will like her better or it will improve the chances of getting a job, we have to remind her that she should be doing it for herself."

If people come in with unrealistic expectations of what they will look like after the procedure, the surgeons explain the procedure cannot be done.

Kevitch has patients sign a consent form to insure they know what the possible outcomes of the procedures are.

Iyer says he does not perform procedures on people who want the surgery "spur of the moment."

There is also a concern if a boyfriend wants his girlfriend to get the procedure done or if he is willing to pay for it. So Iyer says he relies on his "gut feeling" to determine if the potential client has the right motives in mind.

A correct motive for surgery is if someone is "tired of seeing her face in the mirror that looks tired all the time," Iyer says.

Men are more likely than women to have unrealistic expectations of facial surgery outcomes, Iyer says. When men point out what they dislike about their face he becomes concerned. This behavior however, is common and almost expected of women who are more conscious of their appearance, he says.

One of the latest trends is giving plastic surgery as a gift, according to AAFPRS. Mothers and daughters as well as couples are having procedures done together, AAFPRS reports.

The requirements for 'ageless beauty' are not the same for men and women.

Cosmetic surgery cannot give someone a "perfect" face, the ASPS Web site informs. Instead surgery improves features people already have.

As the availability of elective cosmetic surgery increases so have the number of younger people seeking this type of surgery. Elective cosmetic surgeries performed on patients 18 or younger increased 48 percent from 2002 to 2003, according to the ASPS.

A new nose for a daughter's 16th birthday is problematic,

Meade says. It sends the message that it is "right to tie self-esteem to looks," Meade says.

Appearance differences should be accepted rather than ignored or made the same.

A New Face?

However, some people desire an entirely different face. Perhaps even a famous face.

Shows such as MTV's "I Want a Famous Face" illustrate society's desire for a perfect (famous) face. In this show, people allow MTV to document their pursuit of a famous face through cosmetic surgery.

Makeover shows "put the spotlight on plastic surgery but downplay what could go wrong," Iyer says. "I worry about patients who come in with pictures of famous people and want to look like them."

Although rare, there is a "potential risk with every procedure," Iyer says.

Along with health risks, there also are satisfaction risks associated with the outcome of a cosmetic procedure. Surgery may not always turn out exactly how the patient expects it, Iyer says.

Surgeons point out what surgery will do for a patient, Kevitch says. Patients should "lie flat on their backs and hold a mirror up, gravity will tell what we can do," he says.

The similarity between faces may increase with the possibility of facial transplants in the near future.

This type of surgery would use a face of a cadaver and surgically implant it onto a person who suffers serious facial deformities from a fire or an accident, Dr. W.P. Andrew Lee, the University of Pittsburgh Medical Center's chief of plastic surgery, told the Associated Press in July [2004].

Kevitch says face transplants are a wonderful option for people who are seriously disfigured. He says it will never become a possibility in elective cosmetic surgery.

For now, more animal tests need to be done before facial transplants become a reality for the seriously disfigured, Lee says.

Iyer fears facial transplants will become a possible cosmetic procedure.

"What's fiction today is reality tomorrow," he says.

6

Women's Magazines Drive the Demand for Cosmetic Surgery

Deborah A. Sullivan

Deborah A. Sullivan teaches sociology at Arizona State University. She is the author of Cosmetic Surgery: The Cutting Edge of Commercial Medicine in America, *from which this viewpoint is excerpted.*

Many women's magazines have promoted cosmetic surgery by publishing articles that emphasize the benefits of various cosmetic procedures while downplaying their health risks. One of the reasons for the growing number of articles that describe cosmetic surgery in a positive light is pressure from surgeons who use public-relations campaigns to influence the writers and editors at women's magazines. A survey of articles about cosmetic surgery in women's magazines reveals that many journalists portray cosmetic surgery as a cure for "genetic deformities" such as wrinkling skin, flat or average-sized chests, and round thighs. Such articles encourage women to regard their own faces and bodies as deficient and in need of medical "correction." Many articles further suggest that cosmetic surgery transforms women's lives and brings them happiness. The marketing of cosmetic surgery in women's magazines continues to grow.

[Research provides] evidence that physicians regard women's magazines as one of the most important sources of the public's ideas about cosmetic surgery. Survey data support this belief. The first major battle in the intraprofessional turf war was caused by an article that appeared in *Harper's Bazaar*. The American Society of Plastic and Reconstructive Surgeons' recently initiated national advertising campaign relied heavily on women's magazines. Public relations efforts by this organization and the others involved with cosmetic surgery, more often than not, target women's magazines. These specialty organizations work aggressively to influence the content of articles and other editorial copy. They pressure writers to include their referral numbers and, more recently, Internet sites. They want more than only a complimentary promotion. They want to manage the media message about cosmetic surgery to promote public demand for their services.

> *They want to manage the media message about cosmetic surgery to promote public demand for their services.*

Women's magazines participate in the cultural construction of appearance as a medical problem. While advertising also influences ideology, the messages are usually more limited due to space restrictions. Special advertising supplements would be an exception. Magazine coverage, in contrast, is much less restricted. It is also free and carries an aura of greater legitimacy. Consumer surveys have shown that people prefer media reports to ads as sources of information. This is why the American Society of Plastic and Reconstructive Surgeons (ASPRS) until recently spent more on public relations than advertising. Individual physicians continue to turn to public relations services either as a substitute or supplement to advertising campaigns. Typically, they pay monthly retainers of fifteen hundred dollars to firms in the Midwest and to small firms elsewhere. Monthly fees to larger firms on the East or West Coasts can reach six thousand dollars. Physicians recognize that public relations are an important part of marketing an elective medical procedure such as cosmetic surgery.

Articles about cosmetic surgery in women's magazines provide readers an opportunity to learn physicians' ideology about the problematic nature of body parts that fall short of the cultural ideal. They instruct readers about the medical interventions available to alter their appearances, who is an appropriate patient, and what are realistic expectations about the surgical experience and outcomes. They also provide a forum for physicians to advance their position in the turf war. . . .

An Analysis of Magazine Articles

Reader's Guide to Periodical Literature indexes the content of periodicals by topic. Cosmetic surgery entries are listed under "Surgery, plastic," "Liposuction," and "Breast implants." *Reader's Guide* only indexes articles, a policy that excludes brief discussions of cosmetic surgery in the ubiquitous, composite medical-and-beauty-advice columns and letters to the editor in women's magazines. Moreover, *Reader's Guide* does not index *Women's Day* and *Family Circle* or new magazines with small circulations. As a result, the 173 articles listed in women's magazines from 1980 through 1995 constitute a large sample of the cosmetic surgery articles in them, rather than the full set of such articles. Two published in *Sassy* were not available for coding, yielding 171 articles for analysis. In spite of these limitations, this set of articles encompasses the large bulk of the discussion of cosmetic surgery in women's magazines available to readers over the sixteen-year period.

The articles were read numerous times to identify common themes and characteristics that were then used to code their content. The aim was to describe the content of the articles as fully as possible. Although much of the thematic content echoes the themes of the ASPRS's Public Education Program, begun in 1977 and expanded in 1982, the content analysis of the articles was completed before the author was aware of this program.

Types of Cosmetic Surgery Articles

Many of the 171 articles discuss more than one surgical procedure. Procedures often are grouped according to their common aesthetic goal, such as changing the profile by modifying the shape of the nose, chin, cheekbones, and ears or reducing the outward signs of aging with eye, brow, and facelifts or with skin treatments. Because some procedures are frequently done at the same time, each article is classified by whether it discusses at least one of the procedures in each broad category. For example, an article about nose modification, ear pinning, chin extension, and thigh liposuction, is coded only once under the "profile" category and once under the "body contour" category. Chemical peels, dermabrasions, and fat or collagen injections are separated from eye lifts and facelifts because the latter two can involve altering musculature and bone structure while the former only involve skin. Breast reduction is distinguished from augmentation because most physicians and patients argue that the primary motivation for the former is functional, not cosmetic. Breast reductions are included, nonetheless, because there is still debate over the "need" for this elective surgery.

A few cosmetic procedures occur too rarely to code as a separate category. These include a short 1993 *Ladies' Home Journal* article on penile augmentation, a 1994 *Ms.* article lambasting *First for Women* for an article promoting cosmetic genital surgery for women, and two *Vogue* articles on lip augmentation in 1989 and 1995. Lip augmentation is mentioned briefly in several other articles. Earlobe trimming and scalp reduction are each mentioned once in articles focusing on other procedures.

> *The increased coverage of cosmetic surgery both reflects and contributes to readers' interest in medical procedures to enhance appearance.*

Three formats dominate. The most common is the instructional guide or update that promises to answer readers' questions about the latest methods and new trends. Nearly two-fifths of the articles fall into this category. These usually provide an overview of the clinical aspects of one or more procedures and costs, along with a typically cursory mention of potential risks and, sometimes, a discussion of how to determine whether you are a good candidate and/or how to choose a physician. Another one-fifth are autobiographical accounts that also mention the motivation for considering cosmetic surgery. These have become increasingly common; nineteen are indexed from 1990 through 1995, compared to fourteen in the 1980s. The third format, also encompassing about one-fifth of the articles, is much like the first except the discussions of procedures are personalized with a description, often accompanied by quotes, of the experience of at least one former patient.

Both the autobiographical articles and those that include the experiences of real patients give readers the opportunity to identify with someone else's discontent about some aspect of her body and consider her solution. Some titles encourage this identification by asking, "Does Your Face Need a Lift?" "Is Liposuction Right for You?" "Breast Reduction Surgery: For You?" or, when multiple procedures are reviewed, "Cosmetic Surgery: Would It Work for You?" "Cosmetic Surgery: Yes or No?" and "Will Changing Your Looks Change Your Life?" Others try to catch the readers' attention with clever titles like "A Stitch in Time," "Eye-Opener," "Waist Not," "Fast Curves," "Getting It Off My Chest," and "Future Perfect." Some of these also have a sidebar or subsection inviting readers to consider whether they should undergo cosmetic surgery.

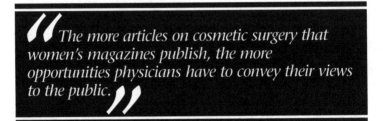

The more articles on cosmetic surgery that women's magazines publish, the more opportunities physicians have to convey their views to the public.

About one-fifth of the articles do not fit in any of these formats. About half of these are about the breast implant controversy. They are discussed in a separate section. The rest range widely from articles on post-operative care and makeup, video imaging, and cosmetic surgery in the Soviet Union to the results of surveys about cosmetic surgery and two "best" lists of practitioners.

Anti-aging eye, brow, and facelifts are the most frequently reviewed cosmetic operations. *Vogue* and *Harper's Bazaar* average more than one article a year. Articles on breast implants are a close second, pushed up in rank by a flurry of articles between 1989 and 1993 in response to the Food and Drug Administration's actions to restrict access to silicone-gel implants. Procedures that modify the profile of the head are mentioned next most often, followed by body contouring through tummy tucks, buttock and leg lifts, and liposuction.

Physicians' Expert Advice

Physicians play a major role as medical experts in the articles. They provide information on the technical nature of the cosmetic procedures and define appearance as a medical problem requiring treatment by an appropriately qualified physician. They also provide information on risks and benefits as well as appropriate motivation and realistic expectations of outcomes and reassure readers that cosmetic surgery is a healthy choice. With the exception of nine autobiographical reports and thirteen others, including seven on the breast implant controversy, a 1989 *Good Housekeeping* reprint of an ASPRS press release on "Who Gets What" cosmetic surgery, and the 1991 *Glamour* survey, all articles include physicians as authorities. Most directly quote or paraphrase physicians and provide their names, cities, affiliations with hospitals, medical schools, centers, institutes, or physicians' organizations, and titles of published books, if any. Ten are written by or with physicians or excerpted from physician-authored cosmetic surgery consumer guidebooks.

The number of physician names appearing in the articles ranges as high as 71 in a list of cosmetic specialists in *Harper's Bazaar's* 1984 "Who Does What Best." Most articles only cite 1 to 4 physicians. A total of 422 are named in the 171 coded articles in addition to the 71 on the *Harper's Bazaar* list and another 27 on a similar 1981 *Good Housekeeping* list. Some names reappear in numerous articles, others in several, while still others are mentioned only once during the sixteen years of the sample. . . .

Medicalization of Appearance

The inclusion of physicians as authorities in the articles contributes to the medicalization of appearance as does the increased number of cosmetic surgery articles. The increased coverage of cosmetic surgery both reflects and contributes to readers' interest in medical procedures to enhance appearance. A 1991 *Glamour* article reports that nearly three-quarters of readers who responded to a survey in a previous issue say that they think the boom in cosmetic surgery is "fine—people should do whatever they feel is necessary to improve their looks." Perhaps more telling, 29 percent of the respondents say they already had cosmetic surgery, 33 percent expect to within the next five to ten years, and another 9 percent say they may when they are much older. Liposuction, breast enlargement, and nose modifications are the procedures most often contemplated by those thinking about cosmetic surgery. Although such voluntary responses are far from representative of all readers they provide editors with support for the expanded coverage of cosmetic surgery. The more articles on cosmetic surgery that women's magazines publish, the more opportunities physicians have to convey their views to the public.

Cosmetic surgery's obvious attraction is its potential to modify appearance to more closely approximate the current ideal. The articles remind readers, "Like it or not, no one can dispute this fact: In this image-conscious world of ours, looks count," as a 1988 *Teen* article says. Some go further and link cosmetic surgery to a moral endeavor. For example, a 1988 *Mademoiselle* article quotes a physician who claims that "youthful beauty, in our culture, is equivalent to good and ugliness to bad." A psychiatrist in this same article suggests, "Patients may unconsciously think of it as baptism by immersion—you go in with your sins around your neck and come up out of the water reborn." A previous 1980 article by two physicians in this magazine argues that even a "relatively minor imperfection, evident to no one but ourselves" cannot be tolerated: "We reject emphatically the fatalistic assumption that there is virtue in tolerating what we perceive to be imperfect.". . .

The tone of most articles is relentlessly positive and sometimes lighthearted.

Articles frequently refer to cosmetic surgery as a cure for genetic "deformities," even though the attributes labeled as deformities fall well within the normal range of physical variation or age-related changes. For example, liposuction is referred to as a way to cure the contour deformities due to heredity. Nose, chin, and ear modifications and breast augmentation and reduction are similarly presented as treatments for genetic deformities, while facelifts and eye lifts are touted as cures for a "genetic predisposition to wrinkling" and "under eye bags.". . .

Articles Downplay the Risks

The tone of most articles is relentlessly positive and sometimes lighthearted. A few examples include *Ladies' Home Journal's* "I'm in Love—With My New Face," *Good Housekeeping's* "The Happiest Decision I Ever Made," *McCall's* "Cosmetic Surgery for Real Women," and *Women's Sports and Fitness's* "One Woman's Liberation." The major exceptions are twenty-four articles exclusively on breast implants, published after the FDA began a review of implants in 1988. . . .

Only eight other articles emphasize the risks of a cosmetic operation more than the benefits. One is *Mademoiselle*'s "4 True Tales of Plastic Surgery," in which two tales are negative: a shocking story on breast implants and a subsequently corrected nose job that left a patient temporarily disfigured. Another is *Glamour*'s 1988 "The Cosmetic Surgery Hoax," which focuses on health risks and poor aesthetic outcomes as well as the turf battle over cosmetic surgery. Despite only presenting negative examples of cosmetic surgery, it concludes, "Not all cosmetic surgery turns out badly. Most of it turns out pretty much as planned." Moreover, it contains a sidebar, "How to Check up on a Cosmetic Surgeon," which implies that serious problems can be avoided if readers select their physicians carefully.

The other articles in which the presentation of risks overshadows benefits focus on one kind of surgery. These include two on facelifts in the same 1981 *Harper's Bazaar*, one on liposuction in a 1989 *Vogue*, a personal account in a 1991 *Good Housekeeping* of a woman left with pain, a distorted face, and nerve damage from silicone injections to build up her cheekbones, and the 1994 *Ms.* article criticizing *First for Women* for promoting female genital surgery. The *Ms.* author dismisses the *First for Women* article as a "dreadful piece in a dreadful magazine." But, she also claims that other "smarter" women's magazines "venture onto the same slippery slope" by minimizing the risks in their enthusiastic coverage of cosmetic surgery. She further chastises them for playing on women's insecurities, encouraging women to become self-absorbed, and feeding women's worst obsessions.

Negative articles on facelifts, nose modifications, and liposuction stress the unreliable aesthetic results more than health risks, as do a few generally favorable articles on these and other procedures. For example, 1989 and 1995 *Vogue* articles on lip enlargement and other discussions of collagen, fibril, and fat injections into acne scars and facial creases, although not advising readers against the procedures, stress the temporary duration of change, a matter of two or three months. Many articles on facelifts or eye lifts similarly note that these changes are not permanent, but the duration is measured in years, not months. A few others, including a fairly negative personal report of a facelift in a 1986 *Ms.* and a report on liposuction in a 1993 *Essence*, offer cautionary tales. These articles stress the need to select a qualified physician or express concern about trying to find self-esteem through surgery.

Approximately 35 percent of the articles tell readers nothing about the health risks of cosmetic surgery other than, in some articles, the temporary side effects common to any medical procedure—swelling, discoloration, numbness—and the potential for infection. Another 16 percent say that there is a possibility of other complications without specifying them. The 28 percent of articles that briefly mention specific risks, such as potentially deadly reactions to anesthesia, nerve damage, facial paralysis, vision problems, or blood clots, dismiss them as rare and typically stress the importance of physician selection, as mentioned in a previous section. Only 22 percent discuss health risks in sufficient detail to emphasize cautious consideration of the possibility of physical complications, as well as choice of physician, when thinking about cosmetic surgery. The eight articles judged to emphasize risks more than benefits fall into this last category along with others that provide examples of good outcomes and patients who are happy with their cosmetic surgery. . . .

Social and Economic Benefits

Despite some titles that suggest otherwise, none of the articles promises that cosmetic surgery will improve your life. Many explicitly state that it will not solve life's problems, or save a marriage or a job. However, some of these same articles, as well as others, suggest that it could make a difference; they discuss former patients whose lives were transformed or who say simply that they are happier now. Some of these women talk about the misery of being teased for their big breasts, nose, or ears as teenagers, or about their obsession with their fat thighs and ankles or flat chests. *Better Homes and Gardens'* 1993 "The Healing Power of Plastic Surgery: It's More Than Just Skin Deep" offers a good example of the mixed message. The authors say, "Modern medicine may improve your appearance, but it won't solve your other problems," only two paragraphs after quoting a dermatologist who claims, "I've seen patients who were afraid to leave home. . . . When their skin problems were corrected, their lives turned around."

Several articles claim that the benefits sought vary by sex. *Harper's Bazaar's* 1991 "Youth Lifts" opines that women are driven to cosmetic surgery by "romantic desires . . . wanting to maintain their appeal to husbands or mates," whereas men's "impetus is business-related." Articles in *Working Woman* disagree. The 1988 "Career Woman's Guide to Cosmetic Surgery" says, "Many high-achieving women—even those who previously shunned the concept of cosmetic surgery as frivolous—are beginning to wonder whether a straighter nose, a stronger chin or more youthful-looking eyes could translate into increased dollars and success in the marketplace." Moreover, the article notes that surveys indicate, "many people believe a youthful appearance and physical attractiveness are key ingredients for achieving power and success on the job." Six years later, "Face Value" provides numerous examples of professional women, celebrities, and several well-known feminists who have had cosmetic surgery. The author informs readers about the economic studies that find men and women who are rated below average in attractiveness typically earn less than those rated above average. Although the author warns that the positive changes some patients experience may be secondary effects of enhanced self-confidence, the author also notes that "[i]n an era in which corporations are slashing budgets and laying off older workers," readers need to be concerned about their image.

> *The marketing of cosmetic surgery in women's magazines continues to increase.*

The message is the same in magazines aimed at a minority audience. An African American surgeon in a 1991 *Essence* article comments, "Society is saying that you cannot be successful if you're not good-looking. Many things are based, and many assumptions are made, on how you look. It's not fair, but it's true." Surgical modification of racially distinctive features, although increasing, remains highly controversial. This article warns that friends may accuse cosmetic patients of racial self-hatred. However, the chief of plastic surgery at Howard tells readers that this pathological motivation is only true for 10 to 20 percent of patients and suggests that they will be better served by a physician who shares their cultural background and understands their desire to soften a prominent feature or beautify themselves, not make themselves less African American. . . .

Everybody's Doing It

The normative nature of cosmetic surgery is the last of the dominant themes evident in the articles in women's magazines. Readers are reassured that cosmetic surgery is a morally, socially, economically, and psychologically appropriate choice. For example, a 1985 *Vogue* article points out, "the demographics of plastic surgery have shifted: no longer are patients only movie stars or the super-rich; they are also stockbrokers, executive secretaries, lawyers, school teachers, even members of the clergy . . . who want to look better, less tired, refreshed." Overall, 62 percent of the articles explicitly mention how popular cosmetic surgery has become among people like the readers or provide statistics to convey this impression.

The proportion of articles providing specific examples of women who have elected cosmetic surgery has increased from 44 percent in the 1980s to 70 percent from 1990 through 1995, excluding those on the breast implant controversy. Most are middle- and upper-middle-class white females. Only four articles focus on men and only the two *Essence* articles discuss African Americans and Hispanics. Reader identification is further enhanced by mentioning their ages, which mirror those of each magazine's readership.

The desire to surgically alter appearance is treated as normative for teenagers as well. Teen and preteen readers are told, "More and more teens are choosing plastic surgery. That's why *Teen*'s talked with some great gals who've put their faces (and figures) in the hands of plastic surgeons—and couldn't be more pleased with the results." *Seventeen* tells them not only that "there's nothing wrong with wanting to improve your looks," but also, "If [your parents] are unsympathetic (and some are), a teacher, minister or counselor may be able to reopen the discussion.". . .

The marketing of cosmetic surgery in women's magazines continues to increase. A new magazine designed specifically for women interested in cosmetic surgery, *Form and Figure: The Future of Beauty*, debuted in 1998. The ASPRS targeted women's magazines in its 1997 and 1998 national campaigns to advertise cosmetic procedures. Following the successful strategy of pharmaceutical companies, manufacturers of cosmetic surgery devices began advertising directly to consumers in mid-1999. The first ads were for breast implants and were placed in women's magazines and on television and radio. The number of breast implant surgeries are once again increasing rapidly.

7

Patients Can Become Addicted to Cosmetic Surgery

Virginia L. Blum

Virginia L. Blum is an associate professor of English at the University of Kentucky. She is the author of Hide and Seek: The Child Between Psychoanalysis and Fiction, *and* Flesh Wounds: The Culture of Cosmetic Surgery, *from which this viewpoint is excerpted.*

Some cosmetic surgery patients become addicted to plastic surgery, certain that the next operation will perfect their appearance. Whether the surgery turns out well or not, these patients continue to want more. The woman whose husband has been cheating on her may believe that with just one more cosmetic procedure she can return to the girl he was once faithful to. However, surgery provides only temporary relief for feelings of emptiness and dissatisfaction. After each surgery, even if patients are happy for a while, they will soon find another part of their body they want to "improve."

When you look in the mirror and begin to imagine the imperfect part traded in for the improved version, you cannot help but see your body as in need of or lacking the pretty jawline or upper eyelid. The economic aspect only underscores the flows of exchange, deficit, possession. You buy a nose.

What did it cost you?

Did you get what you paid for?

Did you find love through the new body part? A partner? Does your mother love you now? Your creator?

Your surgeon?

So what are the consequences of becoming surgical? The lifetime effects? . . . Some people have a few carefully spaced surgeries—say, a teenage rhinoplasty, a thirty-something eyelid lift, a fifty-something full face-lift. Others may start much later but then pursue it with intensity—like a patient I interviewed who began with her eyes in her late fifties and took it from there. What are the combined circumstances that might lead to a "plastic surgery junkie"? Or is there any difference, really, between the person who undergoes repeated procedures and the one who simply has incorporated a moderate surgical schedule into her or his life?

In the Beginning

I observed the rhinoplasty of an eighteen-year-old girl whose preoperative nose appeared, well, uneventful. It was small, regular in shape, no humps, no bulges. I felt surprised. As it turned out, another surgeon had refused to operate. I can't imagine *anyone* twenty years ago performing surgery on this girl's nose. No, she didn't have Candice Bergen's nose, or Christy Turlington's, or anyone with that very narrow hyper-Anglo-Saxonized nose that registers perfect on the American aesthetic meter. She had a regular nose. But its failure to be paradigmatic, a "model" nose, somehow disturbed her enough to have it operated on.

This is normal. Twenty years ago the attempted refinement of normal features into perfect ones would have been the province of actors—not ordinary people, who would never expect to be evaluated so closely. Now that we've started to appraise our own faces and bodies with the carefulness formerly reserved for screen actors, however, all of us seem to have flaws. Should we be correcting them? Each and every one of them? We only need turn to the host of magazine articles discussing what once would have been dismissed as "minimal defects" to know how far we have come. Moreover, how does it make us feel to see ourselves blown up on the big screen of our anxieties? Can any single surgery solve what drives us? Two or three perhaps?

This is a far cry from the "Jewish nose" that stood out as different from the "American nose" and sought assimilative invisibility. [Professor and author] Elizabeth Haiken has documented that many midcentury recipients of nose jobs weren't Jewish but were mistaken for Jews once they immigrated here—as though the "Jew" was difference itself, a difference emblematized in any nose weighing in as too big. Similarly, as Haiken shows, features linked to blackness, such as large lips and wide noses, were potentially racializable traits that white people would correct because of their aesthetic guilt by association.

This is a different landscape. Although white, Anglo-Saxon, Protestant aesthetic standards still reign over Western society's sense of proportion and contour, racially variegated traits are in style as long as there's just a smattering—large lips, say, or exotically slanted eyes—adding a sensual but controlled irregularity to otherwise strictly Anglo features and skin tone. Large noses can "work," and there are far fewer ethnic noses being bobbed. Features that used to be considered worrisome because of their *racial* valence have been supplanted by a whole new category of the slightly imperfect. . . .

During my postoperative interview with the rhinoplasty patient, she said she liked cosmetic surgery and had no doubt that some day in the future she would have additional procedures, such as rejuvenating surgeries. She contrasted the simplicity of surgery with the protracted experience of braces. "You wear braces for two or three years. With surgery, you go in, and two hours later you wake up different."

> *Twenty years ago the attempted refinement of normal features into perfect ones would have been the province of actors.*

Joan Kron describes her own first experience with plastic surgery (a face-lift) as so gratifying that she went for more surgery five years later—another face-lift, endoscopic brow-lift, rhinoplasty. If "it turns out well," she notes, "you will very likely want more." What I am saying is a little different; you could very well want more regardless. Indeed, if it turns out badly you are stuck wanting/needing more. Kron's own account of her two face-lifts five years apart seems naggingly less than straightforward. Why so soon, I might ask? She offers excuses. She was over sixty, and her doctor said that face-lifts after sixty average only five years of stopping the clock. She was having additional procedures (the brow, the nose, her sinuses), so why not go in and "tug" the lift? Her genial doctor threw in the redone lift for free, referring expansively to warranties and expiration dates. The fact is, she's misleading the reader. In reality, five years is a bit past warranty. Since Kron frequently publishes on plastic surgery in mainstream magazines and is well known by these surgeons, her second surgery should more accurately be called complimentary. I wonder just how successful that first surgery was. Reading between the lines, hers is a typical surgery story; she was escorted halfway to her dream face, where she had that rapturous glimpse; but then when the swelling subsided, skin and muscle reverted. It would be much harder to lose what you had momentarily possessed. In a mournful panic, you watch as the spell dissipates.

Farrah's Face

"Look at Farrah Now" urges the headline of the 4 July 2000 issue of the *National Enquirer*. I look at Farrah's face and don't recognize her. In her place I see a generic post-op woman, plumped up lips, cheek implants, one eyelid hiked a bit too high, profile with a particular surgical lilt to the tip of the nose. Nothing like Farrah. The article explains that eight years ago Farrah "had work to smooth wrinkles and sun damage." Later, after the breakup of a relationship, claims the *Enquirer*, she had a brow-lift. Subsequent to her performance as Robert Duvall's wife in the film *The Apostle*, she received many "offers of work." "And she was convinced plastic surgery was responsible." So why not even more? "When Farrah landed the role in 'Dr. T and the Women,' as Richard Gere's wife, 'the last thing she wanted was to look old and tired in her close-ups. So, she had a major overhaul,' added the insider." True or not, this is the story of surgical addiction— and why, once you believe that surgery "works," you will keep doing it.

If her life isn't better, then that must mean she needs another face-lift.

Farrah supposedly need more surgery to play Gere's wife. It's not just actresses playing the role of the wife who have surgery to keep their faces in check for the hellish close-up. It's also wives who desperately take arms against their faces and bodies to keep their husbands "interested." It's not just actresses who struggle to hold the camera's affection. It's also ordinary women (so many of us) who think that what makes us worthwhile, worth anything, is a pleasing physical appearance. Joyce D. Nash, a psychologist, recounts what she terms a case of surgery addiction:

> Often the surgery addict feels she is fighting a war of attrition with her looks. This was the case for "Barbara." Although Barbara claimed her age was 48, she was actually 54. Despite her blonde hair, endless array of skin creams, and frequent shopping trips for new clothes, Barbara was having difficulty holding her marriage together. Her husband (age 55) was a wealthy businessman who traveled around the world and had casual affairs whenever he could. . . . Barbara had had her face lifted twice in attempts to remain youthful, and while these interventions were technically successful, they never altered her worried and guilty manner. She was very attached to her plastic surgeon, always bringing flowers for his secretary and returning regularly to have the state of her face checked by him.

Nash, who herself had a face-lift, is here trying to distinguish between a normal concern with keeping up one's appearance and the desperate plight of poor Barbara, who blames her aging body for her bad marriage. But Barbara has imbibed thoroughly the cultural lesson about the necessity for women to look good. If her life isn't better, then that must mean she needs another face-lift. Comparing Barbara's story with Farrah's, we have here two different but related plastic surgery addiction narratives: Farrah's is the race against time. In one less than vigilant moment, all might be lost. Barbara, on the other hand, thinks she might have a happy life if she could just get it right this time. If this straying husband was faithful early on in the marriage, then it must be that she is no longer the same. She will go to her plastic surgeon and place her face in his competent hands. He will take care of her—even if her husband won't. Why is Barbara doing this? we might ask. Doesn't she realize that no amount of surgery will transform a chronically unfaithful husband into the picture of fidelity? But she has found another man now, her surgeon, who will restore to her these lost treasures. Losing the love of the camera might feel no different from losing the love of the husband. This is where the surgeon comes in—to rescue the fair princess, unlock the crone body in which she's trapped, release her to her real and happy life. She takes her bow. She is loved once again. Waves of love wash over her, just as [movie character] Eve Harrington imagines.

It would be hard not to become addicted. It would be hard to stop once you found out it worked. It would be equally hard to stop if you believe it should work and you just haven't yet found the right formula, surgeon, procedure. Whether it's for reconstructive or purely aesthetic reasons, the ongoing sense of imperfection pushes us forward.

The Pressure to Look Young

It is important to understand and come to terms with the psychology of these practices, because then we are in a better position to know what drives us. Moreover, we need to think about the relationship between our personal practices and culturewide trends and transformations. It is true that as more and more of us begin to change ourselves surgically, our distinctions, our variations will be less obvious. Consider, for example, a world in which, by fifty, every single one of us has had rejuvenating surgery. When surgery becomes the standard of what fifty looks like, what might it mean to refuse surgery? In a culture where younger people have a better time in all respects, why wouldn't you want to look young—given the chance? Perhaps such possibilities strike us as frightening *because* they are so very tantalizing. One surgeon put it all very crisply: "We live in a very competitive culture, and you start looking old and saggy, everybody stops talking to you. I did a very large liposuction two days ago on a seventy-year-old woman. She had just gotten back from a motorcycle trip. She's seventy years old going on thirty, and there are a lot of them out there. You know, they're healthy and they're young and she's going to live to be 110. When you're seventy and you think you've got another thirty, forty years, you don't want to sit on the porch and rot. You want to stay in the game." Somehow, when he puts it this way—that in order to "stay in the game," more in the world, you need to have surgery—it all begins to sound rather coercive. The practice I or my friends or my family engage in for our personal gratification and sense of urgency seems simply like a choice of one sort or another, albeit a choice made in the context of powerful social forces. But what happens when those social forces become so very powerful that no one dare resist them without risking total exclusion? You will be fired from your job and replaced by someone "tidier"; you will be replaced by the youthful-looking at dinner tables; your partner will leave you for someone better maintained; your children will be embarrassed to bring their friends home to see their out-of-control parent; you will for all intents and purposes be socially dead. The rest of the crowd, who are with the program, as it were, will act as though they are among the living. . . .

The Slippery Slope

A friend who has had several rejuvenating surgeries sat across the table from me and asked which surgeon I would recommend for further surgery and what she should have done this time. I was surprised, because, frankly, she looked wonderful—better than she had looked for quite some time. In part, what was nice about her appearance was that her last face-lift had relaxed somewhat, loosening the early post-op stiffness. I didn't know what to say, but I wanted to help. What would do it—her brow? she wondered. No, her brow looked fine. Everything was perfect. Any more and she would look too pulled. But it was clear as she pointed to each sector of her face that there was no satisfying her now. One woman told me that even now, after two face-lifts, every time she looks in the mirror she thinks about her chin—a little tuck, some kind of intervention. But then she turns away—no, not now, not yet. As a consolation, she will have the laser zap her spider veins. And the young woman with the rhinoplasty, whose tip will be just as slender as she ordered, will have future surgeries on that nose for several reasons. One reason is that she didn't ask for what she really wanted, which was an entire new nose. So concerned was she to appear absolutely reasonable, a person who knew what she wanted—yet moderated by a sense of limits—that she would never have divulged the whole truth of her deepest desire for something like what swoops down from the midface of [actresses] Michelle Pfeiffer or Jody Foster. These thin, straight, slightly uptilted noses were what she had in mind, but she wasn't going to expose (no, not for anything) the length and breadth of her yearning. Next time she visits a surgeon, however, she will ask for a little more—which won't seen quite as far from the surgical nose she now possesses. . . .

You would be crazy not to be operated on when doing so will change your life—you will be loved, you will be successful. You would be crazy to refuse all that. Yet this very same surgeon, in another mode, explained quite emphatically the difference between the normal patient and the pathological: "I spend at least an hour talking to people before surgery. And while on the surface I'm just getting information about the operation they want, I'm also doing a psychological evaluation. How stable is this person? What is their true motivation for doing this? Why surgery now? I have one fellow who returns to me every year. He comes back to see me because I'm the only one who won't operate on him. I think that his concern needs to be dealt with not through plastic surgery but through therapy—that's what I've told him. And he comes back after he's had another two surgeries."

Whether it's for reconstructive or purely aesthetic reasons, the ongoing sense of imperfection pushes us forward.

"There *are* people who are overly narcissistic. There are people who are overly concerned with their appearance. . . . I turn away thirty percent of cosmetic patients," boasted one surgeon, while another surgeon claimed a turn-down rate of "one out of three." But no one I know and no one I've interviewed has been turned away—ever—by any surgeon. . . .

The Fix

I said to my friend, face it, you will never be entirely happy with what you look like. Surgery will make it better for a short time; then it will seem all the worse. She replied that I was right, that for a time it does its work and you feel great even though you already scrutinize the defects—eyes that aren't quite even or a bulge you thought would flatten entirely—and then later it doesn't look good at all, and you need another fix.

Surgery temporarily gratifies the hole in your narcissism that requires attention *some place*, and why not start on the surface if you can't locate the "interior" unconscious origin of the demand for repair. By the way, let me be clear that when you decide you want surgery to correct what you perceive to be a defect on your face and body, the defect feels quite real. It's not as though a little dose of self-esteem could ever be expected to vanquish those crow's feet or, more important, caring about those crow's feet.

Once you have surgery you will either have it again or want it again. I know two people who have assured me, after a face-lift, that they would never have one again. One has gone on to have several other surgical procedures. The other is very recently post-op. Studies are insufficient; they don't track people. Patients go to different doctors for their multiple surgeries, and so no one knows or traces the surgical circuit. Even people who claim to adore their surgeons often visit other surgeons, because when the nature of the subject is a certain experience of perfection, it's hard to believe you've found it in either the result or the surgeon. It is a circuit that takes you from one doctor to the next, from one procedure to the next; for a while you are exhilarated, as you wait for the beautified part to emerge from the swelling, and then you are back to the mirror, the drawing board of your desire. . . .

The Perverse Cycle of Addiction

They are called delicate self-cutters, most often adolescent females who cut their skin in moments of intolerable anxiety. They make shallow rifts across the surface of their skin. [According to psychoanalyst Louise Kaplan,] "The cuts are carefully wrought, sometimes simple parallel lines but also intricate patterns; rectangles, circles, initials, even flowerlike shapes." These cuts can be a work of art, elevating the body from what is felt to be its abject changes (menstruation, for example) and longings; they can reassert the distinction between the inside and the outside. At the same time, the cuts can function as counterphobic responses to a sense of internal mutilation. The delicate self-cutter becomes herself the agent of a mutilation she dreads passively experiencing. . . . Kaplan observes that "a perversion, when it is successful, also preserves the social order, its institutions, the structures of family life, the mind itself from despair and fragmentation." Like many who undergo cosmetic surgery, Kaplan's perverts experience a deep-seated shame that needs correcting and feel defiant rather than guilty about their perversion, which they nevertheless take to be a violation of the moral order.

58

The surgical patient's shame is intolerable, the thing that drives her or him to the doctor—aging or ugliness or just not being quite beautiful enough. Just outside the operating room, a surgeon explained to me that the patient inside was the "ugly duckling" of her voluptuous family. She was now in the middle of divorce and wanted to improve her appearance. Who can imagine her shame? How can I express the shame I felt for her as her surgeon pronounced the shameful "truth" of her unloveable body.

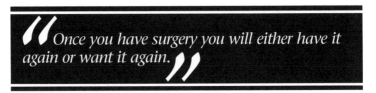

Once you have surgery you will either have it again or want it again.

The genetically blessed, hypertoned, strategically lit bodies of actresses can induce shame in the woman with an ordinary flesh-and-blood body. But even the "real" actress's incapacity to maintain such a body is humorously treated in Mike Nichols's film *Postcards from the Edge.* Actress Suzanne overhears the head of wardrobe complaining to the director about the difficulties of tailoring clothing for the actress's out-of-shape body. They can't put her in shorts because the top of her thighs are shockingly "bulbous." They can't film her on her back during the love scene because her breasts are "out of shape" and will no doubt "disappear under her armpits." They express regret that they hadn't managed to cast in her place another actress whose body was supposed to be "perfect." Many of the women I know, not actresses, just ordinary women, worry about being seen in public in bikinis or short-sleeved tops or shorts rising much beyond the knee, clothes that would disclose to all a shameful and secret part that we keep hidden from view—our flabby thighs, our postpartum middles, our middle-aged arms. Said one surgeon: "I know of many women whose husbands have never seen them nude. I know of women who never go to doctors because they don't want to be seen by them." So, finally they offer themselves up to the surgeon for aesthetic body work, and they are transformed. They can be seen, held, admired. Little by little, we are all becoming movie stars—internally framed by a camera eye.

"The little mutilations take up her mind and enable her to temporarily escape the frightening implications of being transformed physically and emotionally into a woman with the sexual and moral responsibilities of adulthood." Kaplan is writing as though the transition is just one, from girlhood to womanhood, which, for the delicate self-cutter, proves intolerable. What if we were to rethink this universal transition (puberty to womanhood) through the terms of the twenty-first century, where we find the chronological body supplanted by a two-dimensional prototype that is an impossible combination of fashion-centric transitions and age-defying stasis? This is a body always in flux. It can't land on the other side. It can't become and stay comfortably a woman, because it's so difficult and there are always new challenges to face as well as perils to ward off. . . .

And so how different is going under the knife in search of youth and beauty from some ritual and hidden adolescent cutting? Just because the culture has normalized our pathology (of course, it's thoroughly normal to want to look rested and vigorous enough to compete in the youth-centered workplace), it doesn't mean that cosmetic surgery isn't like any other practice that has us offering up our bodies to the psychical intensities that angrily grip us. Ballerina Gelsey Kirkland describes the experience of her initial round of cosmetic surgeries: "The operations found me laid out on a table, yielding to the touch of their probing fingers. I watched my life through the eyes of their needle, penetrating my heart as well as the outer layers of my skin. I would become hooked on the pain, addicted to the voluptuous misery that bound my sexual identity to ballet, to an ever-increasing threshold of anguish." On the operating table, face up, waiting for hands to crawl inside and tug out the ugliness that is like entrails that eventually regenerate and need to be taken out yet again. We struggle up from intolerable bodies vanquished in the exquisite moment of surgical battle in the theater of operations. I recall the scene of a face-lift. One minute she was lying in the swamp of her aging and flaccid skin, and then slowly her face rose from the chaos, sleek, tautened—as though taking shape out of some primal sea—the shards of her outgrown and useless flesh left behind, spirited away by the surgeon's magic.

You will look in the mirror, smile back at the image reclaimed, and relish the grace period between this operation and the next one. The beast-flesh will grow back.

8

Reality TV Shows About Cosmetic Surgery Reveal Americans' Self-Absorption

Psychology Today

Psychology Today *is a monthly journal that explores topics in psychology.*

Reality television shows such as *Extreme Makeover* and *The Swan*, which invite guests to undergo dramatic transformations that include numerous cosmetic surgeries, present an unflattering view of twenty-first-century Americans. The fact that so many people willingly undergo such dramatic procedures suggests that Americans are more overcome than ever with the desire to be recognized and admired. People watch these shows because they see in the participants a reflection of themselves. They watch the transformation of men and women and imagine themselves becoming extremely attractive and winning the recognition of others. This fascination with appearance is so strong because in American society, one's social class and status are not predetermined. It is up to the individual to build an identity and present it to others. However, this focus on one's identity creates a great deal of narcissism.

If a team of alien anthropologists were looking for clues to understand the habits and sensibilities of 21st-century Americans, it could start with the new Fox reality show, *The Swan.* Like *Extreme Makeover*, its predecessor on ABC, *The Swan* invites guests to undergo dramatic self-transformations with the help of fitness trainers, hair stylists, makeup consultants and cosmetic surgeons. Unlike the guests on *Extreme Makeover*, however, contestants on *The Swan* will be prevented from seeing how their cosmetic surgery has turned out until the season finale. In that episode, called "The Ultimate Swan Pageant," 18 surgically altered finalists will compete against one another in a televised, two-hour beauty contest. For the anthropologist, here is an artifact that promises to combine some of the most significant aspects of contemporary American life: grueling competition, the possibility of extreme social humiliation, and plenty of women in bathing suits.

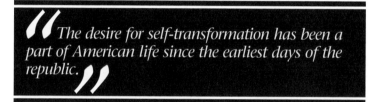

The desire for self-transformation has been a part of American life since the earliest days of the republic.

The fact that so many people eagerly undergo such dramatic procedures (and that millions of people watch them do it) suggests that something deeper is at work here. In fact, the desire for self-transformation has been a part of American life since the earliest days of the republic. How many other countries can count a best-selling self-help author such as Benjamin Franklin among their founding fathers? Cosmetic surgery, once a slightly shameful activity, is now performed at elite medical institutions such as the Mayo Clinic and Johns Hopkins University. According to the American Society of Aesthetic Plastic Surgery, Americans underwent 8.3 million cosmetic medical procedures in 2003. That figure represents a 20 percent increase from the previous year and a 293 percent increase since 1997.

Through the Looking Glass

At the beginning of the 20th century, sociologist Charles Cooley described the American identity as a "looking-glass self." Our sense of ourselves, wrote Cooley, is formed by our imagination of the way we appear in the eyes of others. Other people are a looking glass in which we see not merely our own reflection but a judgment about the value of that reflection. ("Each to each a looking glass/Reflects the other that doth pass," he wrote.) If we are lucky, we feel pride in that imagined self; if not, we feel mortification.

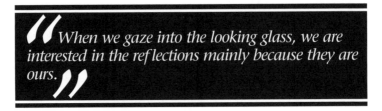

When we gaze into the looking glass, we are interested in the reflections mainly because they are ours.

The metaphor of the looking glass suggests Narcissus, bewitched by his own image, but Cooley did not think that we are entirely self-centered. As he pointed out, we are often keenly aware of the characteristics of the people in whose minds we imagine ourselves. We are more self-conscious about our looks in the presence of people who are exceptionally beautiful, and more ashamed of being cowardly in the presence of the brave. But in the end, when we gaze into the looking glass, we are interested in the reflections mainly because they are ours. "Enough about me," as the old joke goes. "What do you think about me?"

In fact, there is a sense in which Cooley's looking-glass self is built right into our moral system. The moral ideal at work here is "recognition." As the philosopher Charles Taylor has written, today we feel that it is crucially important to be recognized and respected for who we are. This has not always been the case. The desire for recognition is not as important in times or places in which identity is considered immutable and predetermined— where it is part of the natural order, for example, or part of a social hierarchy. We find recognition so important today precisely because so many aspects of our identities are neither immutable nor predetermined. We are not simply born into a caste or social role. We are expected to build an individual identity for ourselves by virtue of how we live and the way we present ourselves to others. Manners, accent, clothes, hair, job, home, even personality: All are now seen as objects of individual control that express something important about who we are.

Recognition = Self-Respect

But building a successful identity cannot be done in isolation. It depends on the recognition of others. And that recognition can be withheld. (You can insist you are a woman, for example, while others insist you are really a man.) Sometimes recognition can be given, yet given in a way that demeans the person being recognized. It's no surprise that from its inception, cosmetic surgery has been enthusiastically employed to efface markers of ethnicity, such as the "Jewish nose" or "Asian eyes." Recognition is necessary for self-respect, and if it is denied, as [African American writer] W.E.B. Du Bois famously put it, one is placed in the position of "measuring one's soul by the tape of a world that looks on in amused contempt and pity." Many Americans have given up on changing the world and have decided to change themselves instead.

> **It's no surprise that from its inception, cosmetic surgery has been enthusiastically employed to efface markers of ethnicity.**

Some people will see shows such as *Extreme Makeover* and *The Swan* as a kind of institutionalized cruelty. After all, they search for contestants whose special psychological vulnerability is an abiding shame about their physical appearance, and then offer them the chance for redemption only if they agree to appear on national television in their underwear. (A Fox vice president, sounding eerily like Nurse Ratched from *One Flew Over the Cuckoo's Nest*, adds that contestants will be put through "rigorous emotional and physical reconditioning.")

Yet there is something weirdly appropriate about cosmetic surgery winding up on television. This may be the logical end point of the looking-glass self. It is not just that people on television are on average much better-looking than the rest of us, though that is certainly true. It is also that the average American spends four hours a day watching television. It would be surprising if all that viewing time did not make us more self-conscious. As the novelist David Foster Wallace puts it, four hours a day spent watching television means four hours a day of unconscious reinforcement that genuine human worth dwells in the phenomenon of being watched. No wonder we can't turn away.

9

Teenagers Should Wait Until They Are Adults to Undergo Cosmetic Surgery

Jae-Ha Kim

Jae-Ha Kim is a staff reporter with the Chicago Sun-Times *newspaper.*

A growing number of parents are paying for their teenagers to have cosmetic surgery. These parents may argue that cosmetic surgery can increase teenagers' self-confidence. However, teens should learn while they are young that their appearance is not the key to a happy life. Furthermore, because their bodies and facial features are still developing, changes that a surgeon makes to their appearance may look strange when they are adults. It is therefore wiser for people to consider cosmetic surgery when their faces and bodies have reached adulthood. It is hard to believe that adolescents would willingly subject themselves to risky surgery in the name of vanity.

Back in my day, a trip to Europe was considered a nice graduation gift. Having your parents pay for your college education was even better. But these days, a growing number of parents are giving girls the gift of the breast augmentation for their Sweet 16 or high school graduation.

In 2003, almost 4,000 girls 18 years old and younger had

their breasts done. I don't think this is exactly what feminists had in mind when they encouraged young women to aim higher.

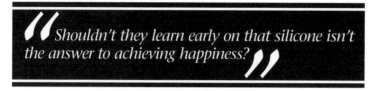

Shouldn't they learn early on that silicone isn't the answer to achieving happiness?

It enhances their self-confidence, some parents may argue. Possibly. But shouldn't they learn early on that silicone isn't the answer to achieving happiness? One day, their bodies will sag and their faces will show the wear and tear of living. Maybe that might be the appropriate time for a little nip and tuck. But at 16?

Parents Are Footing the Cosmetic Surgery Bills

Youth is *so* wasted on the young.

How else can you describe the rising number of teenagers getting plastic surgery to enhance their looks?

According to the American Society of Plastic Surgeons, 9 percent of all chin augmentation procedures last year [2003] were done on patients 18 or under. Think that's shocking? The same age group accounted for 12 percent of rhinoplasty and 60 percent of otoplasty—or ear surgery—procedures. And check this out—21 percent of all male (that's right—male) breast reduction operations were performed on teenagers.

Unless these kids are emancipated minors who have access to huge trust funds, I'm guessing their parents are paying for the procedures and, by doing so, validating that it's OK to go under the knife for cosmetic purposes.

I'm a big proponent that as long as it doesn't hurt anyone else, go for it if it makes you happy. But do teenagers really know what makes them happy? And besides, isn't unhappiness with your looks and general malaise all part of the teen makeup? It's been a while since I was a kid, but I'm pretty sure it is.

It's a shame children these days are so impatient to grow into their faces and bodies. I'm guessing [actor] David Duchovny wasn't exactly a looker as a kid. [Actress] Liv Tyler was awkward and chubby. And even [actress] Halle Berry wasn't Halle Berry–pretty as an adolescent. Most will agree those three grew up just fine.

I look at one of my friends who had a nose job when she

was 13. It's appropriately small, perky and cute for a kid, but on a grown-up face it's dwarfed by her other features. Another pal had her nose done after she graduated from high school. Yes, the doctor made it smaller, but the end result is more of a snout than a nose. Both their original noses were more attractive than their surgically altered features.

Perhaps some of these kids' parents have had a little something done on themselves, so having their kids follow in their footsteps is no big deal. But shouldn't any surgery be a big deal since you can potentially die?

As a kid, I was a fairly decent athlete—gymnastics, track, fencing. And like many athletes, I had my share of injuries. I fell so severely once in gymnastics practice that my doctor had to split my arm open and stick a pin between the broken bones to straighten them before putting my arm in a cast. I also had surgery on my foot, which had been beaten down from years of running.

Having been hospitalized for things that had to be fixed, I can't imagine why anyone would choose surgery when they don't have to. It's not fun. It's not simple. And I think it needs to be remembered that yeah, it *is* a big deal.

10

Doctors Need to Follow Stricter Guidelines in Choosing Cosmetic Surgery Patients

Kimberly Shearer Palmer

Kimberly Shearer Palmer is a graduate student at the University of Chicago's Harris School of Public Policy Studies.

The chief responsibility of doctors is to promote good health, but some cosmetic surgeons are promoting beauty at the expense of health when they advise patients to have potentially dangerous elective surgeries for purely cosmetic reasons. Many patients with psychological problems and low self-esteem choose cosmetic procedures in hopes that they will feel better about themselves when they really need counseling instead. It is wrong for doctors to operate on such patients, yet some do not bother to evaluate their patients' state of mind. Further, cosmetic surgeons do not always explain the risks and possible complications of cosmetic surgery. Stricter guidelines are needed to ensure the safety of patients.

As I waited for a routine skin check at my dermatologist's office, a flier caught my eye. My doctor was offering a special: If a patient organized a Botox party with six or more guests, he would give the organizer free Botox injections and bring complimentary hors d'oeuvres to the party.

His offer may have been generous, but it also was a reminder of a disturbing medical trend: Some doctors have morphed into beauty consultants. Instead of just advising us to get a mammogram or have a questionable mole removed, they now also suggest having a wrinkle smoothed or a breast reshaped. The problem with this role is that it can conflict with doctors' traditional responsibility to promote good health.

Cosmetic procedures don't usually benefit a patient's health; they enhance her or his beauty. The "optimal" treatment is not determined by medical standards so much as by cultural ones. Most professional associations of cosmetic surgeons follow guidelines based on standards set by the American Medical Association. But because cosmetic medicine is elective, stricter guidelines and lower acceptable levels of risk are needed. Doctors need to explain the dangers inherent in any procedure, including making sure the patient's expectations are realistic and he or she is in the right psychological frame of mind for such an operation.

The problem with this role is that it can conflict with doctors' traditional responsibility to promote good health.

The American Academy of Cosmetic Surgery recently announced that its members treated 870,000 patients last year [2003], up 6.7% from 2002. Patients getting Botox injections increased by 11%, and breast enlargements by 8.5%. Even people with youthful skin and bodies seek surgical boosts: Members of the American Society of Plastic Surgeons performed more than 3,000 liposuction surgeries and more than 500 Botox injections on patients younger than 19.

Questionable Ethics

As cosmetic procedures have become more lucrative, some doctors have behaved badly. "We see more ethical violations" in cosmetic surgery, says Rod Rohrich, the president of the American Society of Plastic Surgeons (ASPS). He says the number and details of ethical violations brought to ASPS, however, are confidential.

Indeed, doctors—and patients without sufficient information—are sometimes choosing between health and beauty.

Laser surgery to correct bad vision and eliminate the need for eyeglasses can cause loss of night vision, glare sensitivity and scarring leading to partial blindness, says Betsy van Die, spokeswoman for the Schaumburg, Ill.–based Prevent Blindness America. "Doctors don't always explain the risks and expectations," she says.

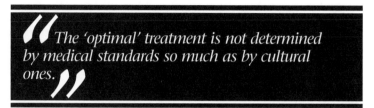

The 'optimal' treatment is not determined by medical standards so much as by cultural ones.

In the most extreme cases, cosmetic procedures can lead to death. Olivia Goldsmith author of _The First Wives Club_, died in January [2004] from complications during face-lift surgery.

Stronger regulations could reduce the risks and keep patients' expectations closer to reality. Steve Miles, a professor of medicine at the University of Minnesota's Center for Bioethics and author of _The Hippocratic Oath and the Ethics of Medicine_, suggests doctors include photos of the long-term effects of cosmetic surgery in addition to the photos of short-term effects, citing evidence that breast augmentations and face lifts tend to look worse with age.

A lack of comprehensive studies on the long-term effects of cosmetic procedures also makes it difficult for patients to make informed decisions. Miles recommends forming a national database to collect information on the effects of all types of implants, including breast and pectoral implants. ASPS does manage a national registry for breast implants, but it is only four years old.

Psychological problems, including eating disorders, also can bring patients into the cosmetic surgeon's office when what they really need is a self-esteem makeover.

Cosmetic Surgeons Should Screen Their Patients

"In the same way that physicians ask someone who is going in for heart surgery if they have a history of high blood pressure, I do think it's important for cosmetic surgeons to screen prospective patients," says Mary Devereaux, who is an ethicist at the University of California–San Diego's Research Ethics Program.

"One wants to know, for example, if the patient asking for liposuction has a history of eating disorders or other severe psychological problems."

Guidelines for two major organizations, ASPS and the American Academy of Facial Plastic and Reconstructive Surgery, do not require doctors to ask patients whether they have a history of body-image disorders.

Stricter guidelines for patients under 21 might reduce surgeries that result from temporary teenage insecurities. Aside from fixing disfigurations, cosmetic surgery should be limited to adults, Miles says: "To sell an operation to a kid, you need to sell them on the idea that their body image is wrong. I don't think it's the kind of pressure we should be putting on kids."

But cosmetic doctors say they only are helping young clients feel better about themselves. "If a kid has big breasts or a bad, ugly nose, they really have psychological trauma. . . . Surgery totally transforms them," says Rohrich of the ASPS. ASPS members performed more than 220,000 cosmetic procedures on patients 18 and younger in 2002. Rohrich, however, agrees that cosmetic surgery is not the best decision for some patients. He says he tells a handful of patients every month that he can't operate on them because they have unrealistic expectations or aren't psychologically prepared.

That's a responsible position. Whether they are getting hysterectomies, tummy tucks or Botox injections, all patients deserve to be treated by doctors who follow the highest ethical standards—which, in some cases, means turning patients down.

Organizations to Contact

The editors have compiled the following list of organizations concerned with the issues debated in this book. The descriptions are derived from materials provided by the organizations. All have publications or information available for interested readers. The list was compiled on the date of publication of the present volume; names, addresses, phone and fax numbers, and e-mail addresses may change. Be aware that many organizations take several weeks or longer to respond to inquiries, so allow as much time as possible.

American Academy of Cosmetic Surgery (AACS)
737 N. Michigan Ave., Suite 2100, Chicago, IL 60611
(312) 981-6760
e-mail: foundation@cosmeticsurgery.org
Web site: www.cosmeticsurgery.org

Since its formation in 1985, the American Academy of Cosmetic Surgery has become the leading representative of practitioners of medical disciplines including dermatology, ophthalmology, plastic and reconstructive surgery, oral and maxillofacial surgery, general surgery, and others. The AACS is the nation's largest organization representing cosmetic surgeons. The academy's purpose is to maintain a membership of medical and dental professionals who participate in postgraduate medical education opportunities, specifically in cosmetic surgery, so that the public is assured of receiving consistently high-quality medical and dental care. Its publications include the quarterly *American Journal of Cosmetic Surgery.*

American Academy of Facial Plastic and Reconstructive Surgery (AAFPRS)
310 S. Henry St., Alexandria, VA 22314
(703) 299-9291 • fax: (703) 299-8898
e-mail: info@aafprs.org • Web site: www.facial-plastic-surgery.org

The American Academy of Facial Plastic and Reconstructive Surgery is the world's largest specialty association, representing over twenty-seven hundred facial plastic and reconstructive surgeons throughout the world. The AAFPRS is a national medical specialty society of the American Medical Association (AMA) and holds an official seat in both the AMA House of Delegates and the American College of Surgeons board of governors. AAFPRS members are board-certified surgeons whose focus is surgery of the face, head, and neck. Its publications include the quarterly newsletter *Facial Plastic Surgery Today.*

American Medical Association (AMA)
515 N. State St., Chicago, IL 60610
(312) 464-5000
Web site: www.ama-assn.org

AMA is the largest professional association for medical doctors. It helps set standards for medical education and practices, and it is a powerful lobby in Washington for physicians' interests. The association publishes journals for many medical fields, including the monthly *Archives of Surgery* and the weekly *JAMA*.

American Psychological Association (APA)
750 First St. NE, Washington, DC 20002
(202) 336-5500 • fax: (202) 336-5708
e-mail: public.affairs@apa.org • Web site: www.apa.org

This society of psychologists aims to "advance psychology as a science, as a profession, and as a means of promoting human welfare." It produces numerous publications, including the monthly journal *American Psychologist*, the monthly newspaper *APA Monitor*, and the quarterly *Journal of Abnormal Psychology*.

American Society for Aesthetic Plastic Surgery (ASAPS)
36 W. Forty-fourth St., Suite 630, New York, NY 10036
(212) 921-0500 • fax: (212) 921-0011
e-mail: findasurgeon@surgery.org • Web site: www.surgery.org

The American Society for Aesthetic Plastic Surgery is the leading organization of board-certified plastic surgeons specializing in cosmetic plastic surgery. ASAPS active-member plastic surgeons are certified by the American Board of Plastic Surgery or the Royal College of Physicians and Surgeons of Canada. The organization provides information on abdominoplasty (tummy tuck), breast augmentation, breast lift, breast reduction, brow lift, eyelid surgery, face-lift, liposuction (lipoplasty), rhinoplasty, and nonsurgical cosmetic procedures including laser hair removal and skin resurfacing as well as injectable treatments such as Botox and collagen. Its publications include the newsletter *Beautiful Choice*.

American Society of Cosmetic Breast Surgery
1419 Superior Ave., Suite 2, Newport Beach, CA 92663
(949) 645-6665 • fax: (949) 656-0249
e-mail: ascbs@mail.ascbs.org • Web site: www.ascbs.org

The American Society of Cosmetic Breast Surgery is a not-for-profit organization dedicated to the welfare of women through cosmetic breast surgery. The purpose of the society is to provide the breast surgeon who treats breast cancer patients a means to gain knowledge about breast implants and how to use them. The organization provides programs for surgeons to teach them how to perform reconstructive surgery on breast cancer patients for very little cost.

American Society of Plastic Surgeons (ASPS)
444 E. Algonquin Rd., Arlington Heights, IL 60005
(888) 475-2784
e-mail: media@plasticsurgery.org • Web site: www.plasticsurgery.org

The American Society of Plastic Surgeons is the largest plastic surgery specialty organization in the world. Founded in 1931, the society is composed of board-certified plastic surgeons who perform cosmetic and reconstructive surgery. The mission of ASPS is to advance quality care to plastic surgery patients by encouraging high standards of training, ethics, physician practice, and research in plastic surgery. The society advocates for patient safety, such as requiring its members to operate in accredited surgical facilities. Its publications include the newsletter *Plastic Surgery Today.*

Austin Smiles
PO Box 26694, Austin, TX 78755
(512) 451-9300
e-mail: ausmile@texas.net • Web site: www.austinsmiles.org

Austin Smiles is a nonprofit organization which provides reconstructive plastic surgery, primarily cleft lip and palate repairs, to people who would have trouble affording cosmetic surgery. The physicians of Austin Smiles perform fifty to seventy-five surgeries annually at Children's Hospital of Austin. Austin Smiles also travels to Latin America to do several medical missions a year.

International Confederation for Plastic Reconstructive and Aesthetic Surgery (IPRAS)
Web site: worldplasticsurgery.org

The purpose of IPRAS is to promote plastic surgery both scientifically and clinically, to further education, and to encourage friendship between physicians in all countries. The organization was founded in 1955 by a group of plastic surgeons who foresaw the need for an international body of plastic surgeons to allow for scientific exchange.

National Women's Health Information Center (NWHIC)
8550 Arlington Blvd., Suite 300, Fairfax, VA 22031
(800) 994-9662
Web site: www.4woman.gov

The NWHIC is a service of the Office on Women's Health in the Department of Health and Human Services. It provides access to current and reliable information on a wide array of women's health issues, including cosmetic surgery. The organization publishes the monthly newsletter *Healthy Women Today.*

Operation Rainbow
3411 Richmond Ave., Suite 333, Houston, TX 77046
(713) 960-7800 • fax: (713) 960-7803
e-mail: info@operationrainbow.org
Web site: www.operationrainbow.org

Operation Rainbow provides free cosmetic and orthopedic surgery to children around the world who do not have access to good health care. They also give ongoing education to health care providers around the world.

Small World Foundation (SWF)
5353 N. Federal Hwy., Suite 301, Fort Lauderdale, FL 33308
(954) 351-4254 • fax: (954) 351-7738
e-mail: info@smallworld.org • Web site: www.smallworld.org

Small World Foundation is a nonprofit organization founded in 1995 to provide reconstructive surgery and medical aid for children and adults throughout the developing world. Since 1995 SWF has conducted three to four medical missions per year to Central and South America and the Middle East.

Bibliography

Books

Jan R. Adams — *Everything Women of Color Should Know About Cosmetic Surgery*. New York: St. Martin's, 2000.

Nancy Bruning — *Breast Implants: Everything You Need to Know*. Alameda, CA: Hunter House, 2002.

Michelle Copeland — *Change Your Looks, Change Your Life: Quick Fixes and Cosmetic Surgery Solutions for Looking Younger, Feeling Healthier, and Living Better*. New York: HarperCollins, 2004.

Court Cutting et al. — *Inside the Minds: The Art & Science of Plastic Surgery—Leading Surgeons from NYU, Georgetown University & More on the Keys to Success Within This Dynamic Field*. Boston: Aspatore, 2004.

Kathy Davis — *Dubious Equalities and Embodied Differences: Cultural Studies on Cosmetic Surgery*. Lanham, MD: Rowman & Littlefield, 2003.

Alan M. Engler — *BodySculpture: Plastic Surgery of the Body for Men and Women*. New York: Hudson, 2000.

Nancy Etcoff — *Survival of the Prettiest: The Science of Beauty*. Lancaster, VA: Anchor, 2000.

Robert M. Freund and Alexander Van Dyne — *Cosmetic Breast Surgery: A Complete Guide to Making the Right Decision—from A to Double D*. New York: Marlowe, 2004.

Joanna Frueh — *Monster/Beauty: Building the Body of Love*. Berkeley: University of California Press, 2000.

Susan Gail — *Cosmetic Surgery: Before, Between, and After*. La Jolla, CA: Melange Unlimited, 2000.

Diane Gerber and Marie Czenko Kuechel — *100 Questions and Answers About Plastic Surgery*. Sudbury, MA: Jones & Bartlett, 2004.

Sander L. Gilman — *Making the Body Beautiful*. Princeton, NJ: Princeton University Press, 2001.

Debra L. Gimlin — *Body Work: Beauty and Self-Image in American Culture*. Berkeley: University of California Press, 2002.

Elizabeth Haiken — *Venus Envy: A History of Cosmetic Surgery*. Baltimore: Johns Hopkins University Press, 1999.

Kathyne L. Jackson — *Dear Diary: What My Doctor Never Told Me About Liposuction*. Bloomington, IN: Authorhouse, 2003.

Michael Kane — *The Botox Book.* New York: St. Martin's, 2002.

Robert Kotler — *Secrets of a Beverly Hills Cosmetic Surgeon: The Expert's Guide to Safe, Successful Surgery.* Beverly Hills, CA: Ernest Mitchell, 2003.

Joan Kron — *Lift: Wanting, Fearing, and Having a Face-Lift.* New York: Penguin, 2000.

Joyce Nash — *What Your Doctor Can't Tell You About Cosmetic Surgery.* Lincoln, NE: iUniverse, 2000.

Adrian M. Richards — *Key Notes on Plastic Surgery.* Oxford: Blackwell Science, 2002.

Ron M. Shelton and Terry Malloy — *Liposuction: A Question-and-Answer Guide to Today's Popular Cosmetic Procedure.* New York: Berkley, 2004.

Naomi Wolf — *The Beauty Myth: How Images of Beauty Are Used Against Women.* New York: Perennial, 2002.

Periodicals

Kirk Baird — "About Face: For Men, Cosmetic Surgery Isn't Just to Improve Looks," *Las Vegas Sun,* August 23, 2004.

Rebecca Bryant — "Reality Television: Are Makeover Shows Changing Perception of Cosmetic Surgery?" *Cosmetic Surgery Times,* June 2004.

Helen Carroll — "I Had Surgery to Keep My Man," *Mirror,* November 2003.

Robert Davis — "Teens' Cosmetic Dreams Don't Always Come True," *USA Today,* July 29, 2004.

Jack Demarest and Rita Allen — "Body Image: Gender, Ethnic, and Age Differences," *Journal of Social Psychology,* August 2000.

Amanda Gardner — "Plastic Surgeons Frown on Reality TV Shows," *Healthfinder.gov,* May 19, 2004. www.healthfinder.gov.

Denise Grady — "Liposuction Doesn't Help Health, Study Finds," *New York Times,* June 17, 2004.

Kelley Kirk-Swindell — "A Lifetime Commitment; One Woman's Account of Her Gastric Bypass Surgery," *Daily Reflector,* February 2004.

Janet Kornblum — "I Wanted to Look Like I Feel," *USA Today,* May 25, 2004.

Liz Kowalczyk and Raja Mishra — "Death Points to Risk of Obesity Surgery," *Boston Globe,* November 6, 2003.

Alex Kuczynski and Warren St. John — "Why Did They Die in Cosmetic Surgery?" *New York Times,* June 20, 2004.

Marisa Kula	"I Got Breast Implants and It Backfired," *Parade*, October 17, 2004.
Lisa Liddane	"Cinderella Wannabes Getting Cosmetic Foot Surgery," *Orange County Register*, July 16, 2004.
Z. Paul Lorenc	"Ten Plastic Surgery Secrets Every Woman Should Know," *Glamour*, October 2004.
Ranit Mishori	"A Whole New Operation," *Washington Post*, December 21, 2004.
Yuri Nakamura, John B. Mulliken, and Myron L. Belfer	"Cross-Cultural Understanding of Aesthetic Surgery: The Male Cosmetic Surgery Patient in Japan and the USA," *Aesthetic Plastic Surgery*, July 2002.
Karen Nash	"Can Cosmetic Surgery Become Addicting?" *Cosmetic Surgery Times*, June 2004.
R. Newell	"Psychological Difficulties Amongst Plastic Surgery Ex-Patients Following Surgery to the Face: A Survey," *British Journal of Plastic Surgery*, July 2000.
Michele Orecklin	"At What Cost Beauty?" *Time*, March 1, 2004.
Maria M. Perotin	"Tourism Companies Luring Americans with Surgery-Vacations," *Billings Gazette*, September 8, 2004.
James Poniewozik	"Trading Faces," *Time*, July 7, 2003.
Yvonne Roberts	"Is There a Woman Out There Who Likes Her Body?" *New Statesman*, May 2000.
Judi Russell	"Getting a Lift," *New Orleans Magazine*, September 2003.
David B. Sarwer, Thomas A. Wadden, and Linton A. Whitaker	"An Investigation of Changes in Body Image Following Cosmetic Surgery," *Plastic and Reconstructive Surgery*, January 2002.
C.A. Stone	"Can a Picture Really Paint a Thousand Words?" *Aesthetic Plastic Surgery*, May/June 2000.
Timothy N. Troy	"Who Is Qualified to Perform Cosmetic Procedures?" *Cosmetic Surgery Times*, August 2004.
Nora Underwood	"Thin Is In—and People Are Messing with Mother Nature as Never Before," *Maclean's*, August 2000.

Index

actresses. *See* celebrities
addiction, surgical
  examples of, 51–54
  narcissism and, 56–57
  normal patient and, 56
  perverse cycle of, 57–59
  pressure to look young and, 54–55
African Americans
  beauty products bought by, 32
  cosmetic surgery among, 30–32
  magazine articles on, 48
  scarring and, 32
Alster, Tina, 17
American Academy of Cosmetic
  Surgery, 68
American Academy of Facial Plastic
  and Reconstructive Surgery
  (AAFPRS), 35, 70
American life, aspects of
  contemporary, 60–61
American Medical Association
  (AMA), 68
American Society for Aesthetic Plastic
  Surgery (ASAPS), 4, 15
American Society of Plastic and
  Reconstructive Surgeons (ASPRS),
  39, 43
American Society of Plastic Surgeons
  (ASPS), 4, 34, 65, 68, 70
appearance
  Asian emphasis on, 26, 27–28
  emphasis on youthful, 33–34
  excessive emphasis on, 6
  medicalization of, 43–44
  standardized ideal of, 4, 5
  white, Anglo-Saxon standards of,
  50–51
  women's magazines and cultural
  construction of, 39
  see also beauty
Argentina, 18
Asia
  aesthetic ideal in, 21
  botox use in, 21–22
  calf surgery in, 22
  emphasis on appearance in, 26,
  27–28
  eyelid surgery in, 19–20
  history of plastic surgery in, 21
  increase in cosmetic surgery in, 20
  liposuction in, 24–25

reasons for cosmetic surgery in,
  28–29
silicone injections used in, 25–26
television programs in, 26–27
"Asian eyes," 63
Aston, Sherrell, 16

baby boomers, 16
beauty
  Asian ideal of, 21
  narrow standards of, women
  conforming to, 35
Beauty Colosseum (TV series), 26–27
Better Homes and Gardens (magazine),
  46
Bihova, Diana, 16
blepharoplasty, 21
Blum, Virginia L., 49
botox, 16
  in Asia, 21–22
  increase in use of, 68
  party, doctor's incentive for, 67
Brazil, 18
breast augmentation
  increase in, 68
  women's magazine articles and,
  44–45
  for young girls, 64–65
breast reductions, 32
burns/burn contractures, 12

Cable News Network (CNN), 17
career, reasons for cosmetic surgery
  and, 4–5, 16, 23, 28, 47
celebrities
  African American, 31
  can induce shame in women, 58
  surgical addiction among, 52–53
chemical peels, 16, 22
children, 12
chin augmentation, 65
China
  financial factors for choosing
  cosmetic surgery in, 23
  leg lengthening in, 5
  plastic surgeons in, 20–21
  reconstruction surgery for child in,
  12–13
Ching Wei, 28
cleft lip, 11, 12
coastal cities, 16–17

78

collagen, 16
Colombia, 11, 18
Cooley, Charles, 61–62
cosmetic surgery
  assessing effects of, 49–50
  costs
    for elective procedures, 34
    parents paying for, 65
    in Thailand, 24
  disasters
    from liposuction, 24–25
    from silicone injections, 25–26
  as gift, 64
  increase in, 34–35, 61
  normative nature of, 48
  public opinion on, 43
  statistics on number of people
    getting, 4
    African American, 32
    gender differences in, 15
cosmetic surgery practitioners
  lawsuits against, 21, 26
  motives for cosmetic surgery
    screened by, 35–36
  patients visit several, 57
  selecting, women's magazine
    articles on, 45
  should screen their patients, 69–70
  in Thailand, 23–24
  turndown rates of, 56
  unqualified, in Asia, 20, 26
Cullen, Lisa Takeuchi, 19

deaths, from surgical complications,
  4
  face-lifts and, 69
  liposuction and, 4
  silicone injections and, 25
Devereaux, Mary, 69–70
doctors
  are becoming beauty consultants,
    67–68
  botox party and, 67
  choose between health and beauty,
    68–69
  do not always explain risks, 68, 69
  expert advice by, in magazine
    articles, 42–43
  see also cosmetic surgery
    practitioners

economy, impact of, 23
Ecuador, 11
Egypt, 5
Essence (magazine), 45, 47, 48
Extreme Makeover (TV series), 5, 61,
  63
eyelid surgery, 16, 19–20, 21, 34

eye lifts, 45

face-lifts
  addiction to, 51–52
  magazine articles on, 45
  men and, 16
  youthful appearance from, 34
facial deformities, 7–13
facial transplants, 37
Fawcett, Farrah, 52–53
feminists, 35
Few, Julius, 18
First for Women (magazine), 41, 45
Fisher, Garth, 5–6
Fodor, Peter B., 5
foot binding, 21
forehead lifts, 34
Form and Figure: The Future of Beauty
  (magazine), 48
Foster Wallace, David, 63

genetic deformities, 44
Glamour (magazine), 43, 45
Glenn, Marcia, 32
Goh, Alvin, 27–28
Goldsmith, Olivia, 4, 69
Good Housekeeping (magazine), 43,
  44, 45

Haiken, Elizabeth, 50–51
hair transplants, 35
Handa, Toshiya, 26–27
Harper's Bazaar (magazine), 39, 42,
  43, 45, 46–47
He Xiaoming, 23
health insurance. See insurance
  coverage
health risks, 37
  doctors need not explain, 68, 69
  magazine articles downplay, 44–46
hernia, of brain tissue, 9
Hirayama, Teri, 28–29
Hispanics, 48
Hsieh, Philip, 21
hymen reconstruction, 5, 22

India, 21
Indonesia, 20, 25
insurance coverage
  face-lifts and, 34
  for reconstructive surgery, 10
Iyer, Manny, 33, 35–37

Japan, 19–20
"Jewish nose," 50–51, 63
Johns Hopkins University, 61

Kaneda, Koji, 26

Kaplan, Louise, 57, 58–59
Kevitch, Robert, 34–35, 36, 37
Kim, Jae-Ha, 64
Kimura, Saeko, 19–20
Kirkland, Gesley, 59
Korea, 20, 22, 24
Kron, Joan, 51–52

LaBelle, Patti, 31, 32
Ladies' Home Journal (magazine), 41, 44
laser surgery, eye, 69
Latifah, Queen, 32
Latin America, 18
lawsuits, against plastic surgeons, 21, 26
leg lengthening, 5
Lin, Jean, 23
liposuction
  in Asia, 22, 24–25
  deaths from, 4
  increase in, 68
Lomax, Courtney, 33
"looking-glass self," 61–62
Low, Karen, 31
lymphatic condition, facial
  deformity from, 10

Mademoiselle (magazine), 44, 45
magazines. See women's magazines
Magee, Kathleen, 7, 8
Magee, William, 7, 8
male-to-female sex-change
  operations, 22
malpractice suits, 26
Mayo Clinic, 61
McCall's (magazine), 44
Meade, Elizabeth, 34
men, cosmetic surgery use by
  in Asia, 22, 28
  geographical distribution of, 16–17
  increase in, 14–15
  influence of television on, 17–18
  in Latin America, 18
  magazine articles on, 48
  reasons for, 4–5, 15–16
  statistics on, 15
  teenagers and, 65
  unrealistic expectations for facial
    surgery and, 36
Midwest, the, 16
Miles, Steve, 69
Morocco, 5
motive(s)
  achieving physical ideal as, 4, 5
  career-related, 4–5, 16, 23, 28, 47
  desire for recognition as, 62–63
  desire to look young as, 28–29,

33–34, 54–55
  desiring face of a famous person as, 37
  doctors should screen, 35–36
  men's, 4–5
  reality television shows and, 5–6
  rejection from relationships and, 5, 53–54
  shame as, 58
  societal pressures and, 4
  vanity as, 15–16
  women's magazine articles on, 46–47
Ms. (magazine), 41, 45

narcissism, 56–57, 62
Nash, Joyce D., 53
Nichols, Mike, 58
nose operations, 50–51, 65–66

Oetomo, Dede, 25
Operacion Sonrisa Ecuador, 11
Operation Smile, 8–13

Palmer, Kimberly Shearer, 67
Park, Chan Hoon, 24
penis-enlargement procedures, 22
Philippines, the, 8–11
physicians. See doctors
Plastic and Reconstructive Surgery
  (journal), 4
plastic surgeons. See cosmetic surgery
  practitioners
Postcards from the Edge (film), 58
Preecha Aesthetic Institute, 24
Psychology Today (magazine), 60

Reader's Guide to Periodical Literature, 40
reconstructive surgery, for children
  in developing countries, 8–13
rhinoplasty, 50, 51
Rohrich, Rod, 68, 70
Rollins, Tanisha, 30–32
Romania, 12
Rosen, Christine, 6

Sakaguchi, Yumi, 27
Samuels, Allison, 30
scars
  in black skin, 32
  from liposuction, 25
September 11 terrorist attacks, 15–16
sex-change operations, 22
silicone injections, 25–26
skin treatments, 16
societal pressures, 4, 33–34, 54–55
Sullivan, Deborah A., 38

Susruta Samhita (Hindu medical
  chronicle), 21
Suwanpradeep, Kawinna, 24–25
Swan, The (TV series), 5, 61, 63

Taiwan, 20
Takasu, Katsuya, 20
Takemoto, Satsuki, 24
Taylor, Charles, 62
Taylor, Miki, 32
teenagers. *See* youth
television
  Asian beauty shows on, 26–27
  cosmetic surgery promoted on,
    17–18
  cosmetic surgery reality shows on
    help people learn about cosmetic
    surgery, 5–6
  institutionalized cruelty on, 63
  reflection of American
    sensibilities in, 60–61
Thailand, 20, 22, 23–24
Tiewtranon, Preecha, 24
Toral, Ruben, 23
Tou, Tsai, 28
transsexuals, 25–26
Troy, Bill, 14
tummy tucks, 30–31
tumor, reconstructive surgery after
  removal of, 9–10

Van Die, Betsy, 69
vanity, 15–16
virginity, 5
Vogue (magazine), 41, 42, 45

Wall, David, 6
Wells, James, 5
women
  ideal for beauty in, 4
  right of, to choose cosmetic
    surgery, 35
  using cosmetic surgery, number of,
    15
women's magazines

articles in
  on benefits, 46
  content analysis of, 40–41
  dominant themes in, 48
  downplay risks, 44–46
  formats of, 41–42
  link cosmetic surgery to moral
    endeavors, 44
  physicians' expert advice in,
    42–43
  purpose of, 39–40
  on reasons for cosmetic surgery,
    47
influence public's perception,
  38–39
pressure from cosmetic surgery
  organizations on, 39
Women's Sports and Fitness
  (magazine), 44
Working Woman (magazine), 47
wrinkles, men and, 34–35
World Journey of Hope, 10, 11, 12
Wu, Woffles, 26

Yamamoto, Hiromi, 28
Yetman, Randall, 16, 17
young, pressures to look, 4, 33–34,
  54–55
youth
  Asia ruled by culture of, 28–29
  botox injections for, 68
  breast augmentation and, 64–65
  cosmetic surgeons should have
    stricter guidelines for, 70
  with facial deformities,
    reconstructive surgery on, 7–13
  increase in cosmetic surgery
    among, 16–17, 36–37
  magazine articles for, 48
  nose jobs and, 65–66
  parents paying costs for, 65
  self-cutters among, 57, 59
  statistics on, 4, 65

Zukowski, Mark, 15–16, 17